# MBA?
# Creating or Running A Business?
# Entrepreneur?

# Then Read This

(Lessons From The Coal-Face)

Norm Hosken

Norman Hosken has asserted his right under the Copyright, Designs and Patents Act, 1988 to be identified as the author of this work.

# Contents

**By Way of Introduction** ............................................................. 1
About The Author .......................................................................... 2
AUTHOR'S PREFACE .................................................................... 3
**Some Business Basics** ............................................................... 9
Start Here ....................................................................................... 10
Always Get It In Writing!! ............................................................ 11
Is There Such a Thing as Free Money? ..................................... 17
Education for Entrepreneuring – Study Law ............................ 19
Bill Gates Dropped Out of University ........................................ 23
Do What You Do Best and Delegate the Rest – But Remember – Nothing Is So Constant As Change! ........................ 24
Make Friends Out of Business / Not Business Out of Friends ................... 27
Minority Shareholding – Things To Watch Out For ................. 28
Intuition: If it Feels Right, Do It ... but Talk to Your Mother First ............. 30
**Planning** ....................................................................................... 32
Plan to Fail by Failing to Plan - Business Planning for Beginners ........... 33
Dashboards – Blow Minds, Enable Buy-In, Generate Consensus and Optimise Time ........................................... 36
Plan to Fail by Failing to Plan - Strategic Planning 101 ......... 40
The Marketing Plan ....................................................................... 47
**The Customer Interface** ........................................................... 50
Initiating Real Customer Relationships - Create Out of the Box Differentiated Customer Impact ............................ 51
Value vs Price ................................................................................. 54

Customer Lifetime Value (CLV) .................................................................56

What Percentage of your Customers are Truly Profitable? Also, Be Aware - The 30% Rule ...........................................................................................59

Target Account Selling – The TAS 1-20 ....................................................61

Churn – Understand The Difference in Value between Winning, Losing and Retaining a Customer ........................................................................64

Rationalising Your Supply Chain – Significantly Reduce Costs But .... Beware the Ying & Yang ...........................................................................66

The Art of the Sale - Discovering Customer Hot Issues .........................68

Getting to 'Yes' – Overcoming Objections to the Sale ............................72

The Customer Agrees the Sale – Say Nothing ........................................73

Squash, Bowling & Customer Relationships ...........................................74

Brand & Branding ......................................................................................76

Voice of the Customer – VoC ....................................................................81

Customer Relationships - Why Fly-fishing Can Be So Important? ............83

**Competition** ...............................................................................................84

Aligning With Strategic Giants .................................................................85

A Way to Neutralise the Competition .....................................................87

**Recipes for Project Success** .....................................................................88

The Customer is Always Right??? Oh Really!! Then Why Do So Many Procurement Projects Fail? .....................................................................89

Optimising Request for Information (RFI) & Request for Proposal (RFP) Procedures .................................................................................................94

**People, Performance, Recognition & Reward** ......................................97

Invest & Reinvest in People – Permanent Staff .....................................98

Invest & Reinvest in People – Contract & Freelance Staff ....................100

Nest-egging Pension Fund Contributions .............................................102

'Wizards of the Week' Awards ..................................................................104
Staff Reviews ...........................................................................................106
Key Performance Indicators – KPIs ........................................................108
Using Peer Review Groups .....................................................................110
**Teamwork** ...............................................................................................112
The Power of Teamwork ........................................................................113
**Negotiations**............................................................................................116
The Power of Honesty and Openness in Negotiations ..........................117
Approaches to Negotiation ....................................................................119
Negotiating – Black Hats & White Hats .................................................121
The Power of 'Open Book' .....................................................................122
**Miscellaneous Tips & Tricks**..................................................................124
Optimising Your Commute .....................................................................125
Nervous about Public Speaking? – Then Try This .................................126
The Art of War – Messages For Business...............................................128
Making Friends With The Media ...........................................................130
Never Get Lost in Translation ................................................................132
Political Risk............................................................................................135
Academia – Your Development Partner ................................................136
Academia – Your Talent Hatchery .........................................................137
Knotty Problems ....................................................................................138
Why Are Some Senior Recruits So Useless But Have Incredible References?..............................................................................................140
Sandwich Bar Economics .......................................................................142
**In Conclusion**.........................................................................................144
Murphy's Law .........................................................................................145

Let's Step Back and Think About Social Media for a Minute ................... 146
And Finally.... ................................................................................... 147
Change, Trust & Timing ....................................................................... 148
Some Additional Thoughts...... ............................................................ 149
Value.................................................................................................... 150
Postscript............................................................................................. 151

# By Way of Introduction

# About The Author

Norman Hosken was born and educated in the UK and on leaving college commenced a career in banking and information technology in the city of London. After several years he emigrated to New Zealand and after stints in banking computing and also several years with IBM, he commenced the creation of a number of businesses nearly all connected with IT.

Eventually from a base in New Zealand he ventured further afield and over the last forty years, apart from new business creation, has undertaken a range of business and market development, consulting and advisory roles internationally within both the public and private sectors, including major project management and advisory roles internationally within the Big 4 Professional Services firms. His business involvement encompasses addressing mainstream commercial business management needs through to developing international marketing strategies for a range of applications and business concepts even including remote sensing from space applications!

His experience incorporates numerous company creations, sales, mergers and acquisitions and he has been appointed to several national and international technology development boards. He has been a speaker at a variety of international conferences and seminars usually on the theme of technology uptake and development and has accumulated business experience in over twenty countries, including funding proposal assessments for and across the EU.

When not involved in the business world he has a passionate interest in fishing as may be evidenced in some of the contents.

## AUTHOR'S PREFACE

In trying to describe this book and what you are getting involved in - on the one hand, and in some respects, this book might be in the same vein as *'what they don't teach you in business school'*[1]. It's based on over forty years of real world and at the coal face business experience. I certainly believe that the contents might provide a useful adjunct for those readers who are preparing for or currently studying for their MBA. On the other hand, a lot of what they do teach you in business school can be crystallised, applied or translated into some very simple but highly effective approaches in the way in which you develop - both your business life and your approach to business. With a bit of luck there may be some gold nuggets herein which might help you avoid some of the surprises and down-sides of what business life can throw at you (forewarned is forearmed). Hopefully there might be a few insights upon which you can capitalise. Those insights are what I am trying to provide you with - in a very straightforward easy to read and assimilate way!

I am likely ancient by most readers' standards. Either way, it's highly likely that I have been around for longer and maybe have developed some wider experience. Irrespective, I will try to be as informative and current as possible.

Overall, remember some Golden Rules.

- Never patronise.
- Always under promise - it enables you to over deliver.
- And, oh yes, never under-estimate that person on the other side of the desk.

There are other Golden Rules too. We'll come to them a bit later on.

---

[1] Do read *'What they Don't Teach You at Harvard Business School'* by Mark McCormack. Much is focused at 'big business' but regardless, very applicable to most situations.

If you are contemplating satisfying your entrepreneurial instincts, studying for your MBA (online or otherwise), have already embarked on the path, are considering starting a business, or are already running one, or simply being part of the business world *'MBA? Creating or Running A Business? Entrepreneur? ........ Then Read This'* can be a backgrounder and part of your tool-kit. But bear in mind that in real life the most successful and certainly the most honest people in business will tell you this........

- it's not always what you know, it's who you know;
- what goes around, comes around;
- capability is often secondary to good luck;
- timing is everything, and
- learn by both your own and others mistakes. (Preferably the latter).

We could dedicate a chapter on each of the above headings, we won't but do keep them very firmly in mind. However, thinking about it, separate chapters might be worthwhile. I'll consider it further and we will see what happens later on.

By the way, this book has rather a long-winded title. I refer to it most of the time as *'Then Read This'* but of course by adding the additional words *MBA? Creating or Running A Business? Entrepreneur?* I might get a few more keyword hits from a search engine. And thus a wider readership. Interesting! Something to consider. We will see!

This book is essentially a series of blog pages, (you might call them chapters or anecdotal headings grouped within logical sections). It contains some hints and wrinkles and hopefully identifies how to avoid some potential 'traps for young players', based on almost a lifetime of practical real-world business experience. It's inclusive of and addresses a very wide range of experiences - of both successes and failures – in a variety of industries and from a variety of countries around the world.

Obviously, the experiences and the understanding described in this volume have been built over many years, including quite a span of time inclusive of which one could describe as 'pre-Google'. Certainly, there are now huge volumes of information freely available on the web, inclusive of templates, models and illustrated methodologies[2]. Make a point to search for these and gain further insights into a massive vault of free experience available to you. And be careful how you click. Your personal data is vitally important! Oh yes, and always read the Terms and Conditions!

If push comes to shove, get out of the house or office, consider spending an hour or two in the real world at the local library or your friendly bookstore in front of the section marked Management and Business – most of them serve coffee these days.

It stands to reason that you are most likely highly immersed in the means with which you can augment this volume's contents - with your likely highly specific knowledge and experience of the power of social media. Not fully conversant with the benefits and pitfalls of social media? Then learn. Fast![3]

Additionally, I really don't want to emulate what is already freely available to you in great depth and in fine detail on the net or written up elsewhere. Rather, I want to consolidate simple, easy to read vignettes which crystallise key messages. Elements that you can get your head around very quickly and could well act as a catalyst for your further reading and research – or, amplification or corroboration of your own experience or intuition. I like to think that you could read *Then Read This* in one sitting, in a single day.In the meantime, remember, I am charging for this book. I'm still in business. However, most of all I really do want to give you great **value**[4].

---

[2] I'll refer to some from time to time.
[3] Interesting reading: Zucked by Roger MacNamee
[4] A vital word especially highlighted in bold and a very key aspect of business as discussed in several chapters within *Then Read This*.

I will try my best. I won't attempt to try and provide justification for the price, I just want you to focus very firmly on the value!! Just think.... if just one piece of my experience can assist you make a decision which makes or saves you time, energy or money then we both benefit. You more significantly than me!! Mind you, you might mention that fact to a friend or acquaintance and that may create a chain reaction – it might go viral!! My royalties could amount to something. Who knows? But if you do find something of value then do drop me a line, I would love to hear! And certainly – tell a friend.

By the way, if you develop an interest in discussing further certain content of this book, do let me know – apart from the fact that I am available for mentoring and advisory consulting projects, I would be delighted to provide further elaboration on any of the topics and themes covered in this book. Just email me on contactthenreadthis@gmail.com

They say that you will learn from your mistakes. It's true, but interestingly enough, you rarely never stop making them. By the way, it's always smarter to learn from the mistakes of others! Always remember that!

By the time you have possibly, and finally, made them all, it's time to retire and go fishing, play golf, learn how to play an instrument, do gardening - even write a book! - or whatever turns you on. (By the way, I certainly recommend that you investigate how the first of these choices might become a major part of your business life!). It never ceases to amaze me how being removed from the day to day pressures of business life ignites new thinking and simultaneously relieves stress. It also provides a simple opportunity to share a common interest (certainly from my own experience you would be surprised at how many people I have come across who would love to learn how to fly-fish) and get involved with all those people that you need to interact with and build relationships in running and making your business successful – lawyers, bankers, advertisers, suppliers, even customers!

I make the apology now that a few more times than occasionally within the text, I might attempt to bring up the art of fishing, using it as a means to illustrate a point or two. Thinking about it, it may also extend my possible market to the multiple millions of anglers around the world. Twenty million alone in the USA at last count!! Potentially one hundred million globally. What a market!![5]

As a serious recommendation – do everything you can to avoid stress. Be aware that it can creep up on you when you are not paying attention. Make it your life's ambition to identify and remove stress from your life. When it comes to 'work life / business life balance', continually appraise your own. Ensure a continuity of objectivity and clarity of thought. These are the foundations of all your decision-making.

So, in summary, the idea behind this set of anecdotes, parables, case studies, vignettes, potted philosophies and real-life adventures is to give you some insight into 'learning from others' experiences, successes and failures' and how you might convert or apply such to augment your MBA studies or plan, start, grow and profit from your own efforts in creating and developing your business. Actually, it might not be your business, in which case you can apply some of the ideas and concepts as an added value contribution to your employer or client – and hopefully further demonstrate your unique value proposition to good effect. Either way, hopefully, the content herein will give you at least some easily digestible food for thought.

The sequence of chapters is not overly scientific, in fact the headings are there more or less in the random order that my mind delivered them. However, it might be interesting to analyse why headings popped out in such a sequence. Maybe there is some subliminal underlying message, maybe some are more important than others! Anyway, this book will hopefully educate, possibly amuse (I apologise now that from time to time I have injected a little humour – what the hell – life's short),

---

[5] You have probably seen the bumper sticker – 'Work is for those who don't know how to fish'.

entertain, enlighten you, possibly even frighten you (not necessarily in that order), overall it should extend your own thinking or amplify or corroborate some of the lessons drawn from your own experiences.

Just be aware that the extent of each chapter is unique. Some chapters go for several pages, others just a few paragraphs. Don't consider that the length of each determines its relative importance. Remember, that sometimes more is less and less is more!!

If nothing else, the enclosed will hopefully encourage you to think sideways and maybe a bit differently.

*Just for clarification: occasionally throughout the book references are made to organisations, products or methodologies which may provide a useful insight for the reader. In no case are the references made as being exclusive and should not be interpreted as such. The author is not recipient of any financial gain as a result of including such references.*

# Some Business Basics

## Start Here

If you are contemplating building your own business then there is a logical starting place. You have an idea or concept, you have deeply engrained optimism and the pre-requisite evangelical passion, the future is just a bowl of cherries and all you really need now is to ensure .............. funding.

So, the very first chapter that follows discusses that issue by means of a personal case study.

However, if you deem that reading 'Business Basics' might be interpreted by you as me teaching you to suck eggs – then jump straight to the Planning chapter and just as importantly, the section on the Customer Interface.

## Always Get It In Writing!!

Bear with me on the following background information, the moral of the story and the key take-aways materialise eventually!

Now, in the old days banks had bank managers who (in those days) were resembling your favourite grandfather with friendly smiles, real offices, offers of a cup of tea and a cheery 'how can I help'. That was the situation with which I was familiar when initially setting up in business. I warned you earlier that I was ancient!

I had started my own business with an overwhelming amount of 'sweat equity', very limited financial resources and no real tangible assets. A bit like Oscar Wilde, I had nothing to declare except my genius and of course my delight in working eighteen hours a day, seven days a week, (should have been a lawyer! In fact at one stage, I studied law and thought seriously about it!). More about studying law later.

Actually, what I did have was a very embryonic, bordering on break-even IT contracting business (with me doing a lot of the contracting) and a great new business idea based on the potential to use an existing customer relationship, the power of my personality, optimising timing and praying for good luck.

Using my knowledge of a very well-known existing customer, based on work I had already been involved in, I could see that they really didn't like the cost or complexity of running their own IT. In fact they were investigating removing their reliance on their existing centralised mainframe computers, replacing them with a network of distributed intelligent terminals. Of course, this would involve a complex, and potentially costly, re-negotiation of contractual arrangements with the incumbent vendor suppliers and the likelihood of a raft of staff redundancies with the associated costs, potential operational disruption and loss of certainty – a classic case of FUD – fear, uncertainty and doubt.

The approach that I contemplated was not that far removed from the environment that we see today – transformation, data migration, off-shoring, outsourcing, re-invention, etc. Call it what you will.

I generated a proposition to take over all their equipment, their IT premises and all of their IT staff, providing all their computing, IT administration and operational requirements using a set of service level agreements (SLAs) that addressed and mitigated all their fears regarding performance and continuity. The proposition also enabled them to establish known costs and potential efficiencies for the duration of their cut-over to a new way of working – which by the way might take five years. In other words, a full facilities management or outsourcing service. And an incredibly profitable business for me both in servicing their needs and establishing the basis of a new line of business so that I could provide outsourced services to a wider range of other customers. There was considerable spare capacity across their computing and staffing base, and of course I would retain all the staff.

Well, it was a complicated business to win and it required more than a year of in-depth discussions and a legal contract of over a hundred pages improved over fourteen separate draft revisions. Each week I would call my friendly bank manager (by the way, he and his wife used to regularly come to my home, play with my kids and show me how to prune apple trees – gee whiz, wasn't banking different then?), arrange an appointment and have a cup of tea with him. I would discuss with him the latest draft contract and update him on how much bridging finance I needed from the commencement of the contract to the point in time when I would have received payment of invoices that met my cash flow and substantiated my profit margin post my break-even point.

We are talking here about a significant sum of money, in my terms bridging finance, in his terms - overdraft. But what the hell, when you desperately need access to funding you can call it anything you like. Extortion or usury in most cases! As an aside, let's just remember that despite all the glossy marketing and 'branding' – (more on that later) banks historically have been basically money-lenders from the beginning of time – never forget that.

With each passing week our optimism that the business was going to be won grew and grew. 'Don't worry about the money' said John (that was his real name), 'this is a great idea and the bank are very happy to support you in your hour of need! We are right behind you'!

Well, guess what? The day dawned when the huge contract was finally signed, sealed and delivered. I phoned John and said I had good news. 'Come and see me immediately' he said. So I did.

Tea in his best china cups was on a tray as I arrived and our smiles were as broad as can be imagined. Over a cup of tea John said, 'well done, I'll phone head office and give them the update'.

'When will my funding be available and when can I start drawing it down' I asked. 'Just as soon as I get the confirmation details from head office', said John. 'When will that be', said I. 'Should be later today', said John.

'OK' I said, we shook hands and off I went to purchase the required cases of champagne.

Back at my office a little later I took a call from John. 'Well', he said, 'I have some bad news, head office won't provide your funding'.

At this stage I won't bore you with the language or the details but I'm sure you can imagine.

I had signed a contract with a major corporation to commence with immediate effect with insufficient funding to pay staff or in fact any outgoings! Worse still, the company without my involvement or knowledge, had rapidly informed their staff of the arrangement and had scheduled for me to address all the staff involved, some of whom were highly unionised!

As it was, the customer had taken my words at face value that my bank would provide all the necessary bridging finance. They had not requested any confirmation of this in writing!! They hadn't checked it out as part of their due diligence!! As it happened, neither had I!!!!

Once the panic attack had passed over me, I phoned my lawyer, confirming my request for a burial at sea. Fortunately for me he chaired a very well-heeled investment committee and he put my proposition to them. Extraordinarily, within 24 hours I had my funding at an interest rate that was marginally acceptable – in truth very acceptable given the circumstances.

What a relief! How lucky was I? To come so far and be let down by my own bank at the final hurdle. To be let down by an organisation with whom I had already built a long history, an organisation who had been informed every step of the way and who, through their bank manager representative, had given me the surety and the confidence to pursue a wonderful piece of business. By the way, they were also a key customer of mine! If only I had known!! I could have organised new ways of rounding in the programming of their systems with links to a numbered account, not associated with my name and in a foreign land, like Panama!! Just joking!

So, what are the take-aways from this potential disaster?

Well, here they are.

Irrespective of what you think the relationship is with your potential funder, including the fact that you are keeping their representative significantly aware of progress, <u>NEVER, EVER commit yourself in the absence of a written document</u>, duly signed by both parties (legally binding the organisation, NOT the individual) and making it very clear what is required and how it is going to be delivered. Establish the criteria which govern the arrangement, know what both sides have agreed to live up to.

NEVER, EVER commit yourself to signing a business agreement unless you really have (or will have) confirmed in writing the financial wherewithal to ensure performance. Although it might seem the very nature of entrepreneurism to take chances, or even gamble on success – think VERY carefully. Don't push your luck, the downside can be horrific.

Another key takeaway – always provide an alternative option if you can. Just in case!!! It's called 'Plan B'.

Always get your ducks in a row. And remember banks exist to distil the difference between deposits and withdrawals. Never forget that. Once they have done that, they are free to do anything they like with the (in fact your) money so that they can make……more money. For them. Despite all the 'feel-good' advertising and marketing, forget all those images of puppies, smiling children, happy couples, travel locations around the world, doting grand-parents and the rest…. they are not your closest friend – believe it or not. Never will be. They will NEVER, EVER put your interests ahead of their own.

Develop a back-up plan. In fact if the business or project you need to fund is lucrative enough, get banks and financiers to compete for your business if you can, play them off against each other to secure the best deal.

Be careful in all your dealings with banks. Don't succumb to the marketing, it can be a tough old world!

Credit Unions can be a good alternative to the mainstream banks and there is a growing wider and diverse funding market out there. Consider crowd-funding for example. Look up Angel investors. Search what local, central and regional public sector funding and business development bodies can offer.

In the case of no support from the conventional funding market, the issue of borrowing from family or friends is a curly one. Basically don't do it if at all possible. If things are successful you will always be reminded that it was 'their' funding which delivered your dream. If things are unsuccessful there is every chance that relationships will be permanently soured.

Another issue is the problem of requesting financial help from friends and family and being turned down. This doesn't do much for your feelings towards them! Also consider the attitude of friends and family who feel aggrieved that you have asked them in the first place and putting them in an awkward situation. Whichever way you look at it, there is no real positive outcome.

Coming back to the issue of obtaining your funding, always develop a potential fall-back position should elements of the prospective deal start to change.

Build a dashboard or an illustrative dynamic xl spreadsheet (originally incorporated in your business plan) so that you can dynamically and immediately identify and demonstrate the effects of change. This is not only valuable to provide insight to others but gives *you* clarity of vision when things do take a turn or could do.

Remember, there's nothing as constant as change!

Postscript on the subject: Always make sure you get it in writing!

A second postscript based on the above experience – the subject of due diligence. Do it! Always!

# Is There Such a Thing as Free Money?

Basically the answer should be 'no', however there are some interesting avenues that can be explored. 'Crowd Funding' as previously mentioned and 'Alternative Financing' have demonstrated that if your idea and business case are strong enough, there are people out there who are prepared to back you and I would certainly suggest that you research this area thoroughly. Google 'Business Funding Options' for a treasure trove of possibilities.

Assessing the market for angel investors and venture capital funders is also a worthwhile pursuit but be prepared to give up a percentage of your equity – sometimes a much larger percentage than you might like!

Additionally, and in my own experience, I have found that there are various Development Boards, regionally, nationally and internationally who are prepared to fund or co-fund projects in a variety of fields. Some linked to the promotion of consortia – typically creating linkages between private and public sector entities, research institutes and academia.

By way of an example, I have even received funding in the past from organisations such as Enterprise Ireland to build proposal bids for projects available within the EU, particularly if you can find potential business consortia partners in Ireland in the commercial and academic spheres. Further funding has also been available to enable development and product enhancement work performed by a variety of academic organisations. In essence providing a direct link to an enhanced R&D facility on a 'win / win' basis.

In fact you could do a lot worse than consider Ireland as a base for your business. The support for enterprise there is very significant and besides – the Guinness is good, people are friendly, the scenery is terrific and the fishing is wonderful! By the way, the weather there is nowhere near as bad as people make out! Most of the time!

Many people consider obtaining funding from friends and family. As previously stated, I would caution against doing this. It may seem like a logical first option but the downside of a refusal is the potential strain on or damage to a relationship. Likewise, if things don't go as planned, failure to repay a friend or relative can have very significant negative impact.

Always consider the availability of funding on a 'what goes around, comes around' basis. Always consider repaying the lender at the earliest opportunity, that way you have created an impression that will certainly hold you in good stead if there is a future need to borrow.

Common-sense really.

# Education for Entrepreneuring – Study Law

When working for a very large household name US hardware vendor many years ago, I was fascinated to see that their annual university graduate hiring procedure focused on obtaining the best and brightest….. zoology graduates!! So obviously somewhere in the depths of their resource profiling, experience had proven that these types were ideal fodder for technical systems and programming tasks. Interesting!

In my personal experience, I firstly consider my own children's outcomes. Eldest daughter: English and Art History graduate. Now enjoying a successful career in finance. Eldest son: Geography. Wanted to design golf courses. Now a very customer focused computer systems engineer technical whizz! Youngest daughter: The exception to the rule! Always interested in fashion and dress-making. What happened? Brilliant university graduate in all things related to the chemistry of textiles, photography, fashion business. Now absorbed in her career within the international fashion industry. Youngest son: Left college early. Short term apprentice pastry-cook, itinerant building work and then erstwhile talented but unsuccessful professional surfer roaming the world. Now a marine fisheries inspector.

Moral of this story is that the foundation of education, in many cases, seems to have no real bearing on the ultimate type of work or eventual profession sought or the level of success obtained. But maybe in the incubation of lawyers. That's feasible.

NB: See the next chapter which case studies dropping out of education!

In fairness it should be stated that the most important issue in reality is ultimately to be involved in something that you are really interested in / passionate about. That way 'work' does not exist and you spend your life in a glorious state of self-indulgence. In hindsight maybe I should have been a record producer or a fly-fishing guide! Is there still time?

However, getting back to the subject matter, obviously if your passion-based backup plan, should your business fail, is built on joining an accounting practice, then study accounting!! But in truth I haven't seen that many both passionate and successful businesses created by accountants. And interestingly, I haven't seen that many passionate accountants!! I've seen a few businesses go broke as a result of highly imaginative (so-called creative) accounting though!

Bearing in mind that the larger accounting firms are more accurately described these days as professional services firms, there is always a chance of being involved in management consulting. Which, by the way, obviously requires a different skill-set to accounting according to the area of specialisation you pursue.

Then there is the old chestnut …. how about an MBA?

The usual response involves considering the overall cost, particularly if seeking an MBA from a prestigious business school. Intensive study over two years might cost in the order of £40,000 or significantly more! Admittedly, you graduate with an acknowledged but generalised theoretical qualification (and also, and often more importantly and valuable, a useful business network of class-mates). However, I believe that this should be considered in the context of two years of practical experience at the coal face or in fact a combination of the two. Ultimately … your choice. There are a number of options open to you with online study at significantly reduced overall costs.

Incidentally my personal business journey has provided a few additional insights.

Business requires that you make a sale in which you 'contract' or agree to satisfy a particular need of a customer. The performance of that 'contract' or agreement is subject to a wide and diverse set of conditions. Not always, but generally, the set of conditions is established in a legal agreement and certainly clarifies expectations of service level performance. Thus, in winning business firstly your proposal must make sense to the customer but secondly you need to build on that confidence and demonstrate that you have thoroughly considered exactly how the need will be satisfied. This involves issues, requirements and responsibilities which impact both you and the customer and such must be very clearly stated. There is also a need to establish what the procedure is should things not go as planned. The performance of the contract or agreement also contains a need to very accurately define a full set of Service Level Agreements (SLAs).

The ability to provide this overall level of thoroughness and clarity of understanding is fairly and squarely in the domain of the production of legal documentation. There is a lot of value in being able to draft the basis of agreements yourself, providing such drafts to external legal expertise for rounding out and signing off. This saves costs and focuses down on the nature of your business – which you know better than anyone else. Why pay a lawyer considerable fees to train him or her in the nuances of your business? But more to the point, having the ability to really understand and think in 'legal responsibility' terms is a great asset and advantage and rounds out your value proposition.

Should at some future time, you find yourself acting as a consultant or advisor to customers in their business relationships with suppliers, or to suppliers satisfying a customer need, you will be able to add value by means of interfacing between the two (or more) parties on the legal issues – often leading to undertaking the role of consultant vendor or procurement manager.

Another thought to consider is that your business in time might grow to the point that you begin to consider selling or acquiring or merging. Legal capability and confidence will be a great asset.

So, if you are considering what type of education might suit you best, both prior to or as you ultimately create or further develop your business, I would recommend a study of law. The pursuit of a law degree or qualification prior to, or even in parallel to, your business endeavours and qualifications really makes sense. But be aware, once you commence to build your business there is every likelihood that you will have (or more to the point, should have) little time for anything else, including study! You will have to time-slice very carefully!

Another consideration...should your business aspirations not be realised (which in many situations is unfortunately the case) then an alternative avenue is open to you. It seems that the world can never get enough lawyers. And do any of us know any down at heel or poverty-stricken lawyers!

Case proven!

## Bill Gates Dropped Out of University

At the time of writing, Microsoft is currently one of the world's largest enterprises in terms of market capitalisation. Not bad for it's founder, an under-graduate computer geek who dropped out of university to spend time initially locked up in a garage.

I do know and have met a small number of highly successful individuals who either dropped out of university or chose not to pursue tertiary education. One such individual once offered me twenty percent of his embryonic business for $20,000. I thanked him for considering me but didn't really see the potential and thus declined. It was a bit of a shame, as several years later he sold the business for multi-millions in cash!

I definitely never devalue the capabilities of such individuals, far from it, but throughout my career I have noticed that luck and timing oftentimes play a very predominant role – both ways!

There are some amazing individuals who have capabilities, insight and foresight beyond belief, and there always will be. What I am saying is that education and business success are not inextricably entwined.

Also, in many instances, sweat equity is often an equivalence for a qualification. Experience likewise is a highly prized possession! Never under-estimate the importance of timing. I have also learned that there is no substitute for good luck!

As a bit of an aside, on the subject of luck, I really like the anecdote involving Gary Player the golfer, who was enjoying a very successful run in a number of prestigious tournaments. Subsequent to picking up the winner's cheque and trophy at yet another venue, he was in discussion with a newspaper reporter who suggested that 'Mr Player was seemingly enjoying a fantastic run of good luck'. Mr Player calmly responded by saying; 'it's funny that, the more I practice, the luckier I get'! Food for thought!

## Do What You Do Best and Delegate the Rest – But Remember – Nothing Is So Constant As Change!

As your business starts to grow you become aware that there are even less hours in the day than you were aware of previously. This means that you are working harder and harder (not necessarily smarter and smarter) to accommodate more and more disparate tasks. These include basically all the administration issues: invoicing, mail, payroll, rental arrangements, banking, finance, planning, forecasting, purchasing, accounting, systems development, personnel, correspondence, etc, etc. All this on top of your involvement in sales, marketing, customer relationships and the rest. Not to mention attempts at eating and sleeping and keeping your personal life and responsibilities on an even keel. You suddenly become aware of the need to bring new capabilities into the business.

In my own experience I enjoyed the 'external' elements of sales and marketing and customer development but as the business grew, I desperately needed assistance to manage the administrative issues and also, given the nature of the business, oversight of the technical workload and the personnel / HR requirements. Although you might delude yourself that you can do everything – in reality that is just a dangerous dream.

So it came to pass that I hired two friends, a technical manager and an administration manager, with the latter also assuming responsibility for the HR / personnel function.

This worked well, quite quickly, and as I could see that the business was growing rapidly, I made a decision to redistribute the share capital to provide for the three of us to have a third of the business each. A sort of 'three musketeers' approach - all for one and one for all! The rationale being that it would provide a solid foundation and allow each to contribute meaningfully to the whole in a sort of bond. After all we were all great friends…weren't we?

It turned into a major mistake. I was always the originator of the business and the instigator of growth. I also worked significantly harder and under more pressure than my other two shareholders. The balance which existed in the early stages of the business development shifted, significantly. It became inequitable – their contribution to bottom line disproportionately low - and didn't illustrate the 'all for one and one for all, three musketeers' philosophy that I had originally envisaged.

To make matters worse, in fact much worse, eventually the company was subject to interest from a variety of firms wishing to buy us out. My choice of acquirer was at odds with my two co-shareholders who voted in favour of another organisation. A key aspect of my choice of acquirer was their interest in recruiting me as the CEO of the to-be-merged business. My two partners had different interests altogether, in fact one of them wanted to retire to the country, the other to pursue the path to self-enlightenment.

As it turned out I was out-voted and although the sale took place and a valuable capital gain was made it was dwarfed by understanding some years later, that if we had progressed with my choice of acquirer, I certainly would have been a major shareholder in an organisation with an eventual $400 million share cap! They also could have had some of that equity and they would still have had the opportunity to pursue their dreams.

Moral of the story (1):

Teamwork is great in the sense of partnership, can be great and quite regularly is. However, always consider the value of your initial aspiration or idea when it comes to the distribution of shares.

Never under-value your own contribution to the business success. Appreciate the roles and contributions of others by all means but never short-change yourself.

Always consider that there is nothing as constant as change, particularly as it affects people relationships over time. Never trust that relationships will remain constant over time.

Distribute shares as a means to buy commitment and to reward effort and contribution but always protect your three 'I's:

- inventiveness,
- intellectual property and
- investment (sweat equity or otherwise).

Hang on to a controlling interest for as long as is humanly possible.

Moral of the story (2):

As referred to in a moment, 'make friends through business but never make business through friends'.

## Make Friends Out of Business / Not Business Out of Friends

I was visiting a museum of vintage cars collected over many years by a very successful engineering entrepreneur. In the entrance foyer was a signboard on which the above maxim had been carefully painted. I still have a mental picture of it and it had a profound impact on me. It's a shame that I hadn't seen it many years previously!!

If you have read the previous chapters you will see that I have had and have witnessed some interesting experiences.

I have built some amazing and life–long friendships out of business. Many of them are still experienced on the banks of rivers or in boats with fishing rods in hand! Or watching sunsets with friends with a decent bottle of wine and some good jazz in the background.

In business there is a big difference between a trusted friend and a business associate. Learn to establish the difference.

There is nothing more to say on this subject.

# Minority Shareholding – Things To Watch Out For

Here's another fascinating vignette! Hired as the CEO of a burgeoning but cash-strapped business the individual had an entitlement to a small shareholding as part of his overall package, although verbally confirmed, it was still not formalised when some time later the private equity company that funded the business discontinued its support. That wasn't really a disaster in its own right, but what happened next was. Unknown to the person in question, in fact without his involvement, some other small external shareholders arranged to 'take the business off the hands' of the private equity company. To appease the CEO, he was provided with a new contract as Managing Director within which a small shareholding was formalised. However, as part of the new ownership arrangements, financial reporting was taken away from him, in fact any involvement with the company finances. Additionally, he was not provided with a directorship and a seat on the board. Essentially his role was changed into one which concentrated on sales, marketing and keeping the technical team pointed the right way.

Basically, but naively, he was initially happy with this - to a degree. He still reported to a Board (of sorts) but time spent on financial matters was significantly reduced to solely future revenue reporting and justification for actual performance.

First signs that something was not quite right occurred when some creditor payments and a staff payroll were missed. Subsequently, slowly but surely, the wheels started to fall off. The new owners didn't have access to the level of funding required (specifically to original expectations) and decided to keep that fact away from our friend and the staff. Eventually the business imploded. The financial losses were significant. Creditors descended on the business and the MD was fire-fighting to appease them, trying to keep the business alive and the staff in jobs.

The key take-aways here are simple. As a shareholder and a senior executive, ensure you have the right (even the responsibility) - and exercise it - to see regular reports on the overall shape of the business. Insist on this.

As an MD, and more particularly as a director (if such is formalised) you have an in-built responsibility to ensure that you are aware of the state of play. There are cases when MDs have been attributed legal blame for the demise of businesses on the basis that their lack of knowledge has been interpreted as negligence. In the case where owners or majority shareholders attempt to shield your involvement from the key elements of the business, especially financial position, then start to smell a rodent.

It is essential that you take every step to protect your own interests particularly prior to any action taken by creditors. Keep a set of notes detailing every event, particularly efforts you have made to maintain the integrity of both your own position and the business per se. Take every action to ensure that you don't go down with the ship.

# Intuition: If it Feels Right, Do It … but Talk to Your Mother First

This chapter is going to be short and sweet. You might think that I am not being serious – I am! You might think that I am being frivolous – believe me, I'm not!!

You may notice how often I refer to the issue of 'trust' in business – or more to the point, the lack of it. Also, how careful you have to be to really protect your own interests.

In essence, in business, you ride your luck. You seek the advice and guidance of and trust a range of professionals, of experts and significantly you trust in your own intuition.

Some might even look to their horoscope. Trust me (pardon the pun) – don't do that!!

My experience has shown – on several occasions – that with the best will in the world you can never get it right every time.

There is one additional aspect of decision-making that you can consider if you can – and believe it or not, it seems to work. And that is to get the opinion of your mother prior to making that really big decision. Putting the proposition in front of your mother will likely require you to significantly simplify and spell out the key elements - which in its own right is a highly useful exercise.

Think about it. Irrespective of the fact that your mother is very unlikely to fully grasp all the technicalities of the decision you have to make, she contributes something that is not available anywhere else.

    1. She will always and without reservation put your interests foremost.

    2. She has the power of a mother's intuition.

3. She is absolutely trust-worthy!!

Where else can you get that combination? And free of charge!! Well certainly not counting a nice bunch of flowers or a box of chocolates!!

Of interest in my travels around Asia, I have come across quite a number of very large organisations where the big decisions in fact are not made within the perceived business management structure. You might be surprised but on many occasions, the really big decisions are put to and made by a matriarchal figure!

# Planning

# Plan to Fail by Failing to Plan - Business Planning for Beginners

I very much enjoy the initial activity of planning a new business, seeing how slowly but surely you are going to make your fortune! I am both a fanatic and an evangelist for both business and strategic planning. There's something special about seeing how positive the future is – or can be! There's something special about building spreadsheets and seeing the business crystallised in black and white. Unfortunately a lot of people see that element as time-consuming and do no more than pay lip service to it.

The old adage 'plan to fail by failing to plan' is a truism.

Building a spreadsheet model of the business is to my mind an absolute priority. It needs to be highly granular so if you are estimating sales, it is just as vital to estimate the full cost of sales, in fact establish forecasts for all of the cost elements that make up each finished product or service. Tend towards ABC – activity-based costing – certainly research the methodology. For each cell created build linked cells that enable variable percentage increases or decreases so that you have very fine control. In this way you can visualise the impact of any change in circumstances which will ripple all the way down to your bottom line. The obvious advice is to be as conservative as possible. This is particularly relevant when you are tabling a business model to third parties, particularly a potential funder. It is always better to under-promise – that allows you to over-deliver!! Third party funders love that type of good news!

When thinking ahead, the first year really needs particularly careful attention, should be very granular and expressed at least in monthly estimates. Year 2 can be described in quarters and Year 3 as a full year or two half years. Mind you, from time to time you may need to make your forecasts post Year 1 more granular. Depends really on the nature of your business and the dynamics of the market that you are in. Don't skimp on details!

A key and vital element of the model must be to establish your cash in bank position – i.e. a reliable cash-flow statement. There is a huge tendency for error in this department if your model only reports gross month-end positions. It's feasible that the month-end cash position can be within tolerance of an overdraft or funding arrangement but during the month your cash position can be significantly lower and usually is. This can create a major problem, loss of credibility from the outset and an opportunity for your bank or funder to pull the rug from under your feet! This must be avoided at all cost. Once again, taking a conservative view is the name of the game. Imagine forecasting monthly sales of say $5,000 and an end of month gross profit position on those sales of $1,000. However, your cost of sales are $4,000 and are in fact likely necessitated prior to receiving the invoiced $5,000 which might take several weeks (or even months) to ripple through. During the month your nett cash position is likely negative. This can compound very quickly over successive months.

An ideal model will contain enough information to allow you to accommodate any variation to expected estimates. Use the model to guide not only yourself but any third parties in understanding the real nature of the business in-depth, at the same time allowing any amount of 'what-if'. This allows you to second-guess situations and build in the essential security and conservatism that are required – and in particular, well-established best and worst-case scenarios.

A personal approach that I have always used additionally is to introduce a simple compounding element which enables the view of 'actual year to date' (YTD) plus 'remaining months budgets', comparing that with your originally forecasted / budgeted 'end of year position' – illustrating any variance by both value and percentage. This provides a significantly more holistic view of performance and an early-warning if the business is under-performing or is likely to do so. It is a very simple thing to portray but not often seen.

Developing a dynamic spreadsheet is one thing but building that information into a dynamic dashboard is something else again and is well worth while considering – for several reasons. So, let's get to that now.

# Dashboards — Blow Minds, Enable Buy-In, Generate Consensus and Optimise Time

Have you ever been in the situation where you are presenting (more than likely using Powerpoint) to or with a diverse group of managers, let's say for planning the development and roll-out of a new product - and discover that the participants can't agree with each other? Each establishes an entrenched and polarised position - and likely divergent points of view. It happens all the time and is a major cause of enterprise disruption (read lethargy), as well as being extravagantly expensive – apart from the frustration and massive time-wasting element – not least is the potential for creating a counter-culture of disagreement.

What usually happens within such a presentation is the chair-person listens to the various points of view and positions and then capitulates by saying something like, 'well it doesn't seem like we are reaching consensus or going to get much further today. Please go away and refresh the presentation based on what has been said today and let's reconvene in a couple of weeks time'.

This basically is a disaster, because it doesn't provide any confidence that the next presentation, whenever that is, will get any further and as my French teacher at college used to say 'time's money'!

To address and avoid this type of situation - consider dashboards – in this particular instance as a means of establishing consensus, generating buy-in, optimising time and even creating a much stronger sense or culture of 'teamwork'.

Using an interactive dashboard (even something simple such as Crystal from SAP[6]) enables the presenter to initially put forward a base case and then sequentially invite presentation participants to provide their inputs, that dynamically (in real time) impact and update the dashboard numeric

---

[6] https://www.sap.com/products/technology-platform/crystal-reports.html

values as well as colour-coded visual elements – which can be pie-charts, bar-graphs, gauges and dials etc. In this way everyone can see their point of view represented immediately and see the associated impact on the business proposition overall. A picture is worth a thousand words!

From experience, using this approach introduces significant harmony. The presentation suddenly transforms into a planning 'workshop' with participants interested in applying a diverse range of their own 'what if' parameters. Essentially this approach can generate accord (or conversely indicate a no-go position) with no one feeling threatened – therefore no entrenched positioning. Everyone plays to their strengths and their knowledge of specific involvement in the business and applies their specialist knowledge. This culminates in the production of a truly holistic view.

In this way the need for delays on decision-making are removed or certainly reduced. The new 'interactive planning workshop' presentation environment created through the use of a dashboard facilitates an understanding across the entire group. By the end of the session a consensus position is significantly more likely to have evolved - with each participant buying-in and more likely to support the proposition downstream. Certainly, it allows a significant opportunity for all participants to see and appreciate the overall impacts both positive and negative and be aware of each party's issues. No more need to revamp the Powerpoint and reconvene two weeks down the track!

It goes without saying that in applying this technique you need to have one attendee responsible for adjusting the cells and parameters and projecting them for the group. It might be an external facilitator but preferably someone within the business.

By way of a simple case study, just imagine a group of telecom managers gathered together in a planning presentation session around the strategic introduction of a new product or service.

In order to offset extreme competition, Marketing has established and costed a new campaign for a new product or service. Based on this, Sales are forecasting new Revenue figures over a period of time, Operations are estimating a large increase in subscribers. So far so good! But hang on – Network are saying that the expected new subscriber volume will swamp existing capacity which will not only cripple the prospected new business but will also negatively impact existing traffic causing customer dissatisfaction, churn and new expenditure for equipment upgrade, plus time delays to solve the problems. How can we handle this?

Consider the factors; the key element being network capacity. How can we price, launch and attract business in line with capacity available. What time and cost are required to re-configure or upgrade the network, given required new expenditure, what impact will that have on future margins, etc. etc. Oh yes, and don't forget the overall cost of sale!

Try solving this dilemma using a Powerpoint presentation. Or in fact a series of separate discussions with each part of the business. Think again about the way in which a dashboard oriented workshop can bring the disparate threads together in a consensus oriented and time efficient manner.

Another major benefit of dash-boarding. We have all heard of and in fact have likely suffered 'death by Powerpoint'. A seemingly endless supply of visuals that (irrespective of their Walt Disney credentials) are accompanied by an interminably droning presenter's soundtrack.

Revitalise the boardroom! Use a dashboard to get the key parameters of the business proposition or situation across and encourage interactive 'what if' – 'what if we don't sign the big contract in July – what does that do to our forecasted headcount, our sales values, our bottom line?' Take these elements and input them to the dashboard model. Observe what happens dynamically.

Pictures are worth a thousand wounds but I believe that dynamic visuals and graphics produced in real-time, which are the basis of dashboards, do more than tell a story, they promote analysis, lateral thinking and interactivity. They also promote involvement and participation and, just as evidenced previously, they have the benefit of converting dull, inert or passive (quite regularly boring) planning presentations into valuable 'workshop-like' sessions which can produce a wide range of new benefits and greater focus. They even tend to keep the audience and contributors awake and interested!

What we have discussed above relates to any type of presentation. In the early stages of you building your business and seeking funding or buy-in from external sources, the use of a dynamic dashboard will always pay dividends in conjunction with and certainly over the use solely of a spreadsheet. It demonstrates that you are both aware of and prepared to accept the impacts of the dynamics of change. It establishes you with an enhanced level of professionalism.

It will likely differentiate you from the rest of the pack.

# Plan to Fail by Failing to Plan - Strategic Planning 101

I like strategic planning and I've done a lot of it, as a facilitator, a chairperson and a participant. What I can say is that strategy planning with a skilled facilitator is really the only way to go. The planning session really does need objectivity and a discipline (and time consciousness) to enable focus on key issues and an avoidance of 'noise'. Also, essentially, there is a real need to provide an environment in which everyone participates. Sometimes there is a need to draw out input from individuals who are reticent due to their perceived lower place in the pecking order or simply just by nature of their personality.

The act of facilitation in strategic planning is also a great opportunity to introduce 'teamwork' into the organisation. Testing and refining how a group of people can enable an outcome, can be made into a great team oriented exercise – if carefully managed. Irrespective, understanding, buy-in and consensus across the group are always going to be essential if your overall business strategic objectives are going to be appropriately established and subsequently realised.

Also, and notwithstanding Microsoft Teams / Zoom based video-conferencing, a major consideration is the venue selected for your planning session. It's best to use a well-lit, well ventilated environment that provides plenty of space for the participants. Preferably the venue should be off-site and a mandatory 'mobile phones off' regime should be enforced. You will need a couple of 'analog' easels of flip-chart sized paper and at least one white-board – or the digital equivalent. Experience has shown that the maximum number of participants is eight.

In the 'new normal' post-Covid-19 world there are likely some big issues to overcome in terms of the physical proximity of participants. Applications such as Microsoft Teams and Zoom, with their virtual meeting rooms, have experienced huge uptake and growth as a result of the needs of social distancing. It is more likely now than ever that planning sessions will need to be based on and enable virtual and distance-based participation. This is going to be a new art form to learn. I don't have personal experience of it in the current climate but have had an amount of video conferencing experience in the past. The two approaches are very different. You are going to need some sage advice on how to use and optimise the new normal, virtual planning session. It is also going to be a very good business opportunity in its own right in terms of facilitation.

Notwithstanding this, I really do believe that where possible planning participants should interact in the same physical location as opposed to the virtual equivalent. There is significantly more that the facilitator can pick up on and can then steer the session to a more positive outcome.

The key thing to remember about strategic planning, regardless of in-person or virtual, is that at the end you really do need to have an outcome that is truly bought into, is practical (do-able) and enables measurement against which your progress and business performance can be managed and viewed. Remember the old maxim – 'you can't manage what you can't measure' and you can't improve on something if you can't measure it.

In the text that follows I want to give you more or less a summary of the various issues and considerations but please do further reading and research, particularly online, where there is a monumental amount of finely detailed information available.

The initial element of the planning session is firstly to deliberate on both:

- 'what is it that we actually do or are about to do'? and
- 'what is our overall Mission Statement; i.e. what are we actually trying to accomplish'?

A facilitator would request participants to firstly input their answers to these questions and then go around the 'room' and obtain individual comments. This is always a fascinating and sometimes a very concerning experience. It often illustrates a situation of disparate or conflicting points of view. Better to know that at the outset and be able to re-establish a common focus! Certainly it will determine a baseline - exactly how aligned, or otherwise, participants' existing thinking is!! Leading a discussion to obtain consensus as to the answers to those questions – and enshrining them as the foundation of our thinking and planning, can only then lead to the next stage which is the Strengths / Weaknesses / Opportunities / Threats (SWOT) determination.

An important feature of facilitated strategy planning is not only to fully establish the SWOT but also to get agreement on the approaches to the multiplicity of diverse issues:

- What are our Strengths? Can we optimise our Strengths / what are we going to do to exploit them?
- What are our Weaknesses? How do we address our Weaknesses / what are we going to do to overcome them?
- What are the Opportunities? Can we optimise the Opportunities open to us / what are we going to do to exploit them?
- What are the perceived Threats and potential Risks to our success? Can we counter current and potential future Threats / how do we mitigate them?

Each of these must be annotated by action plans which specify who is involved, what are the milestones / measurable progress issues and what are the timescales? Essentially this is establishing a set of Key Performance Indicators (KPIs)[7] - both on the business per se and the personnel that are responsible for the various elements of the business - which will govern our downstream activities – and focus!! Thus, we will have the ability to manage and measure (and improve).

In consideration of the elements above, what we now need to focus on are our Goals / Objectives.

---

[7] See the separate chapter on Key Performance Indicators.

These should be considered in both the oncoming twelve months and subsequently at least another one or two years. In fact, the approach might be to set longer term Goals firstly and then on a granular and sequential basis set the earlier elements that when achieved, enable the longer term Goal(s).

As previously, we should then consider our over-riding Key Performance Indicators (KPIs) – or if you prefer – quantifiable and prioritised deliverables and their associated achieve-by dates.

These should be very un-ambiguous as they address a wide range of issues to include such as:

- Number of Opportunities / Prospects Identified
- Opportunities / Prospects Conversion Rate
- Achievable Sales Revenue Targets
- Finance / funding requirements – how much, from who and by when
- Time to market (especially if there are critical development, production or manufacturing issues to overcome)
- Headcount / Resource Levels / Skills Required
- Website Traffic / Visits
- Etc. Etc.

Our next focus area should be on an Industry Analysis:

- i.e. What Industry or line of business are we in?
- What are its characteristics / dynamics?
- What stage is it in?
- Is it growing / transforming? How and Where?
- What are the timescales?
- What makes it a particularly attractive place to be – both now and in the future?

Next in sequence should be an analysis of your main Targeted Customers – by name if you can but certainly by segment and type. What are their wants and needs and how do we provide them with real value propositions? This planning element should also drive your thinking regarding specific Marketing types and approaches. In this area of your strategy planning, I believe that it makes very good sense to introduce Targeted Account Selling methodology (TAS) to a degree (more on this later in a separate heading) and certainly necessitates an eventual link between the two methodologies downstream.

The next stage of the session is to complete a thorough Competition analysis.

- Who are our current and future competitors by ranking / by geography / by segment / by demographic / by product or service line?
- What are the existing and perceived market shares of each of our competitors in each of the above?
- What are our competitors' key attributes / value propositions?
- What are their perceived strengths and weaknesses?
- To what extent can we neutralise their impact? (Also see the sections: Art of War: Messages for Business and How to Neutralise Competition)

Now it's time to develop an initial high-level Marketing Plan. This will both support and focus your overall Strategic Plan but ultimately should be considered subsequently as a separate exercise as a key and in-depth business pre-requisite (and a separate heading in its own right).

For strategy planning needs you should now outline:

- how you will approach your identified market(s) / segment(s),
- how you will turn opportunities into signed-up paying customers,
- and how you will apply the means to ensure profitable customer retention and the avoidance of 'churn' (loss of customers or customer turnover).

By the way, always remember when considering the impact of churn that winning back a lost customer is potentially going to prove much more expensive than initially winning them and retaining them in the first instance. This is discussed in a separate heading later.

By providing details at this time on what you consider is your Unique Sales Proposition (USP) and your approach to Pricing and Distribution Channels you start to bring together the sets of information that round out your Strategic Plan. Also this provides the base of information which enables a comprehensive understanding of what you are about in the minds of everyone concerned, including your senior management (ensuring buy-in) as well as key third parties, particularly banks and funders.

By establishing these high-level aspects now, you create a format and set of headings which will drive your activities later in terms of building your Marketing Plan document in finer detail.

Next the planning session should consider the People and the Team involved in making the Strategic Plan functional and the necessary or potential additional Human Resources and Skill-sets that will or might be required over what timescale and at what cost.

You can now commence to build your Operations Plan which will take each of the individual elements that you have identified above, building them into a logical set. A good approach to building this is to use a Project Plan or Visio format within which you can allocate and specify the resources, confirm responsibility centres, isolate the sequences / timing and also visualise the various inter-dependencies.

The penultimate exercise is now to establish your Financial Plan / Projections. This can best be initially created within a spreadsheet – month by month for year one, quarterly for year two and half-yearly for year three. A good idea here, and as discussed previously, is to consider then inputting the spreadsheet into a dynamic dashboard. Dashboards are much easier on the eye and carry significantly more weight when actually presenting, enabling dynamic changes around 'what if' when elements of your projections / forecasts are questioned or you are reviewing and adjusting to market dynamics and potential future scenarios.

The last task to establish within the planning session (prior to breaking up and heading for the nearest watering hole – (try doing that virtually!!) is to create an Executive Summary. Although the last piece of work required it will in fact become the introduction to your overall plan and will ultimately be read first. It should encapsulate the key issues of each of the above elements to provide a shorthand means of understanding. It should be a short but compelling summary that addresses key, salient points and provides a rapid, thorough understanding to a third party (not only your own guide and focus) of what you are about and how you will succeed.

There are many templates available to you to guide the Strategic Planning process and its desired outputs and I would suggest looking online to get a template and applied methodology that will suit your particular style of approach. Also, by hiring in a facilitator (reference check very thoroughly) you will have the benefit of an approach that has been tried and tested in a variety of environments.

Another issue when selecting a facilitator, ensure that you involve someone who is likely to be sensitive to the dynamics / characteristics / personalities of your team and preferably has a good knowledge of the type of business you are in or anticipate being in. This way you not only benefit from navigating the exercise in an optimum way but you might even get access to some additional knowledge and insight from related experience.

The key take-away however is that prior to embarking on any business, you really must take the time and make the effort to plan.

The old maxim 'fail to plan and plan to fail' is a great truism. Nevertheless, do take a look at the Chapter headed 'Murphy's Law'.

# The Marketing Plan

You should have already considered the outline issues of Marketing within your Strategic Plan. However, there is a separate job to do to fully flesh those elements out. Another issue to consider is that once your initial business is growing:

(i) there will be cases where you might be introducing:

- new product and services,
- new and differential pricing,
- new distribution channel(s),
- associated new market research,
- revised analytics,
- etc;

and each incidence of this will necessitate the production of a new, update to or revision of your Marketing Plan:

(ii) Competition will also have a very significant impact on how you go to market, how and where you are selling – what segments, what differentiators;

(iii) Technology will also impact you - for example, developments in internet activity, social media, data security and so on.

(iv) The business environment: Just think very carefully about the potential global impacts of the Covid-19 pandemic or inflationary or recessionary influences, currency conversation rates, political or regulatory environments.

(v) Your relationship(s) and dependencies on the sources and availability of funding.

(vi) Your supply chain when reliant on third-party provision of elements of your product or service.

There is no firm set of rules here. There is no right answer. Rather there is a significant number of key questions that you must ask yourself relative to your own totally unique situation.

Only you can best identify with which channels and how you want to promote your product or service – what intuitively you feel most comfortable with that will interest your target market(s) – how you communicate your particular 'secret sauce' or level of innovation. There are so many avenues:

- TV,
- Radio,
- Trade Shows,
- Conferences / Events / Expositions,
- Online: (e.g. Adwords, Keywords, paid Advertising, Search Engine Optimisation, Social Media),
- Newspapers & Magazines,
- Sponsorships,
- Editorials,
- Advertorials,
- Press Releases
- Hell, you could even tow a banner ad behind a low flying airplane; Etc.

And in relation to that list:
- Where;
- To whom;
- How;
- When and for how long;
- At what cost;
- How much 'bang you will get for your buck' – i.e. value for money.

There is also a lot to be said about the creation of Joint Ventures and Partnerships. I address this in part in the Chapters on How to Neutralise Competition and Aligning with Strategic Giants.

Again, I don't want to understate the importance and value of doing research on the web to identify the wealth of useful information available to you. Neither do I want to re-establish or paraphrase some of the most useful material that I have gleaned from others. In particular I would refer you directly to some excellent material published on the internet by Forbes, in fact some of the most concise and informative I have seen: *31 Simple Marketing Cheat Sheets For Business Owners That Don't Understand Marketing*. Take a peek at it.[8]

I don't mean that to be condescending, far from it, but the material is highly readable and very comprehensive for anyone considering their Marketing Plan – from the complete novice to the most experienced Marketing Director. There are gold nuggets and aide memoirs there aplenty!

---

[8] https://www.forbes.com/sites/johnrampton/2017/06/24/31-simple-marketing-cheat-sheets-for-business-owners-that-dont-understand-marketing/?sh=54d7a39123ae

# The Customer Interface

## Initiating Real Customer Relationships - Create Out of the Box Differentiated Customer Impact

In the 'face to face' environment (and pre-Google) I often would see a trade magazine or news article or passage in a book that I believed had relevance to a business contact or customer. I would contact the customer and attach to the article or book reference something like: 'I saw this recently and thought it might be of interest'. You might call it a customised 'clippings service'. Some days later, I then had the opportunity to phone the customer and ask 'if the article or text was of interest'. Generally it would be and even if the customer was already aware of the article it still demonstrated my interest and value differentiation. Now that I had the customer on the phone I could then throw in the fact that I would be in the neighbourhood a few days later and perhaps there was time for a quick coffee. Using this approach completely got round the issue of making a 'cold' sales call. I had in fact created a new non-threatening approach to make a request for a meeting. More importantly I was establishing the basis of a relationship based on differentiating my approach to customer service and the identification of value.

In the digitised world there are a number of ways in which this approach can be emulated. Have a think and try it out. From the customer's point of view it is very different to being bombarded with purely sales and marketing messages from an organisation and their 'affiliates or partners'.

Here's a little side-track on the subject of customer relationships and fishing in general. I was once bidding for a very lucrative piece of work and was eventually shortlisted. However the key decision-maker seemed very set against awarding me the contract. I decided that I would try and use what I felt was a final opportunity to have a face to face meeting and conclude my fate - one way or another.

It just so happened that the manager I had to see had a very grand office overlooking one of the most picturesque harbours in the world. It was one of those cloudless summer days and the harbour was sparkling. As I stepped inside the office and shook hands I happened to say spontaneously – 'what a beautiful day, wouldn't it be fantastic to be out on the harbour fishing'!

Well, suddenly the manager who I was in fear of looked up and said 'yes it would be' and asked me did I do a lot of fishing. Well 'yes' I replied and then it turned out that we both had the same model of boat, fished the same stretch of coastline and actually lived only two hundred yards from each other!!! A series of amazing coincidences. On discovering this he suggested that as it was nearing lunch-time we should adjourn to a very nice seafood restaurant on the harbour-side and continue our discussion there. We did, for three hours, on everything you can imagine about our fishing! Eventually we got round to discussing the contract, at the end of which point he concluded that on balance it would be very appropriate to award it to me! My proposal was considered excellent, what had been initially lacking was the 'relationship component'!

We became and still are, many years later, firm friends. We have shared some epic fishing adventures on the high seas, with hopefully more to come. The episode was completely unexpected, particularly so as no prior in-depth profiling research had been undertaken. Never do that again!

The moral of this story is that from time to time there are additional ingredients that can be called into play in the development of a business / customer relationship – that have nothing to do with the business per se. They are what you might call 'intangible' elements and if you can find them or come across them, accidentally as in my case, then thank your lucky stars! Instead of casting your fate to the wind, always think seriously about building an in-depth profile of the person or persons that you need to influence or sell to. Also consider the benefits of using Target Account Selling -TAS (more later) to build up a composite picture in assessing your overall relationship.

Also, never under-estimate the potential power of human chemistry based relationships!!

With the impact of global pandemics and the progressive establishment of online / digital business forms with global customer bases and minimal if any direct (face to face) customer connection, there is an increasing need to think outside of the box in creating the means to customise and personalise your customer interactions and customer value / retention strategies. There is no magic bullet here but think laterally on how you might both differentiate and personalise your customer relationships and more to the point how you could fully differentiate your customer service.

Some more chapters on the Customer Interface follow.

## Value vs Price

Although I refer to the element of Value regularly and in fuller detail elsewhere it's worth emphasising (in fact 'pre-emphasising') here in terms of four issues:

I. the significant transformation of your sales approach that can be created – especially in terms of real competitive differentiation and new business 'winability';
II. the simultaneous up-skilling and improved market credibility of your sales force;
III. the noticeable increase in self-belief and effectiveness of your sales personnel;
IV. the improved impact that is created in terms of your customer or target's perception both of your offering and potentially your uniqueness as an organisation.

Addressing the points above, consider what happens when a potential customer is out to tender for a solution. Once they have created their shortlist, the customer purchasing committee will likely build a Cost Benefit Analysis matrix / Competitive Analysis. Temptation is always to highlight the Costs element. If their decision is based predominantly on Price – and you have already established that this is or will likely be the or a major determining factor – the temptation is to keep your price low to win the business. This both exposes your margin / potential profitability as well as creating a dangerous precedent for future bids – particularly with that customer – and the mindset of your sales team. However, if you establish your bid in terms of the likely **value** of the Benefits of your offering then you can position your bid from 'left field' as the 'value standard' against which other contenders will be managed and assessed; i.e. can your competitors match your overall understanding of the business and in fact enable realisation of the true bottom-line benefit value available. In other words, you supply your pricing details in a format which isolates the customer's measurable future financial returns enabled solely through the uptake of your specific offering.

If proceeding in this way, a pre-requisite is that your sales team must initially research with the customer what it hopes to achieve with the application of your solution. I've found that by providing the sales team with a simple xl tool, they can sit down with the customer and isolate and then quantify where financial and other benefits exist - i.e. a template which drives a conversation with the customer that teases out all of the customer business touchpoints with which your solution comes into contact and impacts. Additionally, there are many areas where a financial return is not immediately apparent, for example the customer's staff 'increased job satisfaction'. This can be addressed in terms of the potential financial value of improved staff retention, reduced training costs, avoided staff replacement personnel agency costs, etc. Other areas where an immediate financial return is not apparent can be similarly addressed.

When benefits / value is distinguished over price then the opportunity exists to essentially hike your price upwards!

Yet another consideration is that you can now introduce a range of longer-term benefits and commence building a true appreciation of Customer Lifetime Value. An area that we will address separately later.

Experience has regularly shown that sales staff, armed with a simple xl tool that enables the above approach, become significantly more effective in establishing rapport with customers and customers feel significantly more comfortable that they are now dealing professionally with an organisation which can seriously provide Value – as opposed to a conventional situation in which the sales person only focuses on making the sale.

It also provides new-found confidence for the sales team that they are now dealing directly with key business issues and significantly enhances their job satisfaction as well as their sales successes.

# Customer Lifetime Value (CLV)

Another aspect of having a proper understanding and focus on Value is the capability to examine the potential for cross-selling or up-selling new and additional products or services to existing customers, which presents a strong possibility for significantly reduced or zero additional acquisition costs – e.g. you might go into a coffee shop initially for an Americano but actually leave with your coffee PLUS two croissants and a piece of carrot cake!!

Building an understanding of the profitability of each customer in Customer Lifetime Value (CLV) terms is essential. Many businesses run into trouble as a result of not understanding CLV and losing their most valuable customers. Many businesses run into trouble because they either disregard the needs and costs of truly profitable customer retention or in fact are servicing the needs of a percentage of customers who are not actually profitable. Having the capability to really examine profitability in CLV terms can sometimes lead to analysing out and strategically opting to shed certain types of customers or possibly re-examining pricing.

In the same light there is a need to fully examine your approach to ensuring customer satisfaction.

For a number of years now there has been an emphasis on fully automating or digitising the customer experience. However, it seems that somehow the approach has been for many organisations to utilise technology to reduce **their** costs NOT to enhance the customer experience. (NB: It seems that many organisations have somehow convinced themselves that their online help and Frequently Asked Questions (FAQ) really does interest and motivate the customer!). It's amazing how such practitioners somehow manage to kid themselves and even portray their new tech-led automation as being something that customers should consider as improved customer service!! Have you tried contacting a business online in a hurry recently? Were you impressed with their caring, rapid, human touch?

Did their offer of an online 'chat' with their 'virtual assistant' fill you with confidence that they really did want to retain your business? Did their almost immediate link into their Frequently Asked Questions do anything for you?

We all have worst case examples of sitting on the end of a telephone, listening interminably to a mixture of music and advertising that we don't want or like. Will we treat our customers like that?

Try if you can to visualise all the events and activity leading up to the securing / acquisition of an initial customer. Although there are different needs and requirements and in fact dynamics in comparing winning and retaining a customer online as opposed to other techniques, there are still a significant number of common steps, all involving costs.

Once a customer is won it's essential to capitalise on your investment and keep that customer for as long as possible. Forever, preferably. This is referred to simply as customer retention.

Imagine a business in which a customer spends on average $100 each month with you – that's $1,200 / year. Then extend that for a potential lifetime of 10 years – that equates to $12,000!!! If you consider solely that your nett profit margin is 40% per month, then over the long term, you are calculating $4,800 to your bottom line. A different kettle of fish from the initial perception of $40 per month!!

That seems ok doesn't it? Essentially all that needs to be done is to keep that customer happy for you to prosper. However, the math also needs to incorporate an understanding of the acquisition costs of that customer.

If the total cost of acquisition is $1,000 then bear in mind that it is going to take you 25 months just to break even!! If the customer leaves you prior to 25 months then you are losing money!!

Additionally, the overall long-term bottom line result is $3,800, not $4,800 as previously considered.

The moral of the story is to ensure that you remain highly focused on the characteristics of CLV. Especially so when considering the potential downside should you lose that customer. Additionally, the re-acquisition costs of the one lost customer can often (and more likely will) exceed the costs of winning a replacement conventionally!!

Take some advice. Prior to introducing any new approach, system or technology that impacts the customer base – think very carefully in terms of what is more important – reducing your costs or enhancing Customer Lifetime Value and most importantly enhancing the customer experience - making and keeping the customer deliriously happy!

In parallel to the above, consider the other aspect of CLV. When bidding for new customers, clearly demonstrate how your solution provides the customer with measurable increased benefit (i.e. value) the longer the customer stays with you. In fact provide some incentives to ensure that this happens. Build this proposition into your overall sales techniques and inherently establish real dis-incentives for a customer to consider leaving you.

# What Percentage of your Customers are Truly Profitable? Also, Be Aware - The 30% Rule

In facilitating an initial strategy planning session, I once asked the CEO and senior management team of a very large and well-known international company 'who are your most profitable customers both individually and collectively as a segment, what do you really know about them and what are you doing to keep them for ever'? The answer to the first part of the question was relatively straight-forward but the second and third parts of the question generated some blank expressions.

So we moved on to identify the 'top ten' customers, firstly in terms of revenue and then the much more difficult task of establishing true profitability. This second part necessitating a thorough understanding of the true cost of sales which became a real concern. And in fact a bit of an embarrassment.

Even on the basis that customers had been retained for many years, the organisation had a poor view of real profitability. Further, they really did not understand how entrenched (or otherwise) they were in terms of customer 'ownership', i.e. loyalty or retention. In fact what really were the characteristics of the customer and what was the level of customer satisfaction.

What was necessitated and thus ensued was a high-level Target Account Selling (TAS) session (see the following section on TAS) which focussed down firstly on the level of relationships, extent, quality and influence that existed across each top-ten customer. It rapidly became evident that in most cases there was potential opportunity for competitors to make inroads into the most highly prized segment of the customer base.

Obtaining regular feedback from customers on a 'how are we doing' basis is absolutely essential. Likewise, developing a real understanding of how each customer perceives the 'value' of the relationship is at the heart of building customised customer retention strategies.

Another insight was the identification of one very major customer whose business represented nearly thirty percent of the company's overall revenue and profitability.

When you consider that your gross position would be deemed highly valuable if you were making a thirty percent margin across the entire business – think of the impact of losing just the one customer that in reality provides the significant portion of the thirty percent!!

Moral of the story: If you arrive at a situation in which one or a very small number of your customers contribute the equivalence of your gross margin – (i) love them to death!! And (ii) mitigate the potential risk by bolstering a secondary bloc of customers that can fill the void if necessary.

# Target Account Selling – The TAS 1-20

Every once in a while you come across something which is so simple, so logical and so effective and completely common sense. In my experience that can be confidently said of Target Account Selling (TAS) methodology. At the heart of TAS is the foundation and summary of the methodology in what has been termed the TAS 1-20 which comprises twenty questions grouped into four segments which you ask yourself (or provide as input to a group Sales planning session) to clarify and assess a sales opportunity. Here are the Issues to deliberate on:

**Is There An Opportunity?**

- Is the Client's Application or Project Defined or Undefined?
- Is the Client's Business Profile Strong or Weak?
- Is the Client's Financial Position Strong or Weak?
- Does the Client have access to Funds?
- Is a Compelling Event Defined or Undefined?

**Can We Compete?**

- Are Formal Decision Criteria Defined or Undefined?
- Is our Proposed Solution Fit Good or Poor?
- Can Resource Requirements for the Opportunity be Met?
- Is the Current Client Relationship Strong or Weak?
- Is the Unique Business Value Strong or Weak?

**Can We Win?**

- Is our Inside Support Strong or Weak?
- Is our Executive Credibility Strong or Weak?
- Is our Cultural Compatibility Good or Poor?
- Are Informal Decision Criteria Defined or Undefined?
- Is Our Political Alignment Strong or Weak?

**Is It Worth Winning?**

- Is Short Term Revenue High or Low?
- Is Future Revenue High or Low?
- Is Overall Profitability High or Low?
- Is the Degree of Risk High or Low?
- Does this Opportunity have Strategic Value?

For each of the above, rate your position against known competitors using a pre-formatted template consisting of a column for each competitor – inputting a plus sign if positive, a minus sign for negative or a question mark if unknown. Alternatively, you could colour-code using green (positive), red (negative) or orange (unknown). For each of the TAS 1-20 questions the full methodology also employs a series of further tests amplified by a number of additional questions that might be asked.

By simply using the basic TAS 1-20 you end up with what I call 'at a glance' portrayals of the situation. Where either '+' and '-' signs are used or particularly colour coding, you can see immediately what your overall position is. As you reiteratively use / re-visit the template over several weeks, as you further analyse the sales opportunity, you can see if you are making headway and improving your position or otherwise.

Using this methodology – even in it's most simple form, allows the development of a standardised approach to qualifying a sale using a format that can be presented ultimately to management or a third party for a decision to proceed or otherwise. In applying the full extent of TAS, and using the basis of common sense and logic, additional nested templates are available which allow costing or determining the degree of fit for each of the tests required. Particularly useful is the 'relationship map' where you identify where in the target organisation you have already established a relationship or alternatively where you have an ability to create such or in fact a need to create special influence.

Just consider the number of deals or opportunities that are pursued that ultimately become loss leaders if won, or consume huge amounts of resources or funding when it is highly unlikely that the opportunity can in fact be won or if indeed it is going to be strategically valuable or profitable.

Many organisations have incorporated Target Account Selling as a concept and embedded it within their own methodologies or Sales software solutions and thus you might come across various options. Irrespective, do have a really good think about adopting at least a simplistic approach – even if that is just a consideration of the TAS 1-20, it really can become a major tool in your Sales arsenal.

Without spelling out the entire basis of TAS herein, I suggest you 'Google' the subject and see for yourself how the methodology might be adopted in all it's myriad forms.

The other thing to bear in mind is that facilitated TAS sessions, just like business and strategy planning, seem to provide the best results and the best optimisation of time.

# Churn – Understand The Difference in Value between Winning, Losing and Retaining a Customer

Ask yourself this question: What is more important, winning or retaining customers?

Obviously you initially have to accumulate customers but subsequently it becomes the priority to keep them! Especially the profitable ones!

Various research projects have attempted to quantify the potential costs of losing and replacing a customer. The entire environment under consideration is generically termed the 'Impact of Churn'. Based on personal experience, in addition to learned research outputs, a majority of organisations do not focus anywhere near enough on the issue of churn and the associated costs of losing a customer, replacing the value of the lost customer or on the costs of re-acquiring the lost customer.

Some interesting 'rule of thumb' data for consideration:

- It can cost up to five times more to replace a single lost customer's revenue (with new customers) compared to retaining that same customer.
- The probability of successfully up-selling or cross-selling to an existing customer is rated in excess of 60 percent. The additional revenue could well be valued at around 20 percent of existing annual customer revenue. Thus a lost customer should be considered not only in terms of existing lost revenue but both existing and future lost revenue.
- Two thirds of new business can be generated by existing customer referrals. A lost customer negates that opportunity value.
- One dis-enchanted customer is likely to negatively influence in excess of ten potential new customers. Consider the value of one

lost customer's revenue now and ten times that amount not available in the future!

The other side of the coin suggests that there could well be a number of your customers that in actuality are not profitable. In this sense it is vital that you have the wherewithal to establish true profitability and where it is clear that it does not exist – either take steps to rectify the situation or alternatively shed that customer – but be very mindful of point 4 above!! Predictively unprofitable customers take exception to being told to take their business elsewhere! We will address that very issue in the next chapter.

Another consideration is to recognise 'churn' when you are forecasting revenues, for example when building business, marketing or strategic plans. Particularly so if the nature of your business involves very large numbers of customers. A third party reviewing your plan will likely have a greater confidence in your forecasts if you actually accommodate a percentage of customer numbers or revenues as being subject to churn.

# Rationalising Your Supply Chain – Significantly Reduce Costs But …. Beware the Ying & Yang

I once had the experience of leading a very significant Supply Chain Rationalisation project where the outcome presented potential savings of some $250 million annually!! This equated to over 10 percent of the annual costs of supply to the organisation.

The reason that such real savings could be enabled was based on the fact that there had never previously been a centralised strategy for addressing suppliers and thus multiple suppliers, each essentially offering the same product or service, were retained – often at very different pricing and sometimes without the availability of Service Level Agreements or in fact – Contracts in any shape or form. To make matters worse, suppliers had been and were being selected geographically by dispersed business unit management with no standardised approach to length of contract, terms of trade, service level provisions or pricing. Many of the supply contracts had been entered into on a 'mates' basis. Overall a very fertile environment for a complete rationalisation!

By building a view across a consolidated general ledger and then identifying each and every supplier to each chart of accounts category, the total impact of the situation could be observed. Thus it became possible after in-depth analysis to reduce down the number of suppliers to each category and introduce negotiation to effect significant reduction in costs by virtue of enabling proportionate increase in the volume / value of supply from the reduced number of chosen suppliers to be retained.

This situation became a major relationship enhancement for those suppliers who could now increase the volume of business with my client. However, a major downside existed in terms of those suppliers who were now rationalised OUT of the business of supply. They obviously didn't share the same enthusiasm!

As it happened, my client was a major utility with existing business relationships with most if not all of their original suppliers; their suppliers were also their customers!!

Now the moral of this story is this: if you are going to upset a very significant number of existing customers who are also suppliers, make sure you have already very carefully established how you are going to manage the fall-out. Certainly, identify the associated potential loss of revenue within the overall cost / benefit calculations of the rationalisation project. In particular, assess how you are going to mitigate the potential damage effected on your brand image / market perception!

# The Art of the Sale - Discovering Customer Hot Issues

I once had the task of building a new industry practice for a professional services / management consulting customer. Although they had been in business for many years, they had virtually nil penetration in any service line in a particular market industry segment. Competitive consultancies had built valuable and entrenched positions in not only the segment but also in the most attractive potential client in the segment. Basically I had to start from ground zero.

Irrespective of positioning I decided and strategized to target the most attractive potential client. The first step was to institute an internal communication to every staff member of my management consulting customer. I requested details of whatever previous business involvement or contact they may have had with the target client as well as asking 'do you know anyone at the target client' – irrespective of whether the contact was business or socially oriented. The email went out to the entire personnel base.

Based on the responses I was able to produce an initial 'map' of the various points of contact and specifically where my starting foray into the target client might commence. Importantly I could prepare the initial stage of building a relationship map based on Target Account Selling (TAS) methodology.

Amongst many others I was able to identify and target a key senior manager potential 'catalyst' and made an initial appointment with the target client's national sales manager using the relationship identified and owned within my customer. After the introduction preliminaries I raised the issue: 'given my customer's globally recognised capabilities in an acknowledged broad range of disciplines, perhaps there may be areas in which valuable contributions could be made to assist your organisation? What are the key areas of concern that you currently have within your own environment that could benefit from specialist external input – particularly if such was provided on a _gratis_ basis for your evaluation'?

After the initial shock and surprise, his response was very interesting: 'Our sales teams are working in a highly competitive and sophisticated market. We seem to be consistently competing on price'. My response to this was as follows: 'If we were to create a set of tools on your sales staff laptops enabling them to run interactive discussions with their prospects in which the tool would identify associated product or service solutions (and most importantly the solutions <u>value propositions)</u> and if we did this for you free of charge, would you be interested? (i.e. if we made an initial inroad into automating the sales pitch and dialogue for your sales people using a standardised approach based on value). Further, supposing we ran a monthly segment in your regional sales meetings to train and demonstrate to sales staff the use of the tool and also to address a range of market issues for your sales force - and we also ran these free of charge, would you be interested'?

The response was extremely positive. He really didn't have anything to lose. The sales manager had never previously been approached in this way. We discussed my rationale; if we could prove our value to his organisation in this initial way, perhaps he would entrust us with other business or certainly invite us to bid on future opportunities.

We proceeded to build the tool-kits (which were essentially simple expert systems) and presented them at an initial sales meeting in which we provided instructions and demonstrated how and why the tools should be used. In this particular case not only were we standardising and quality-proving the sales approaches but we were getting the sales teams to now start focusing on <u>value</u> as opposed to price. This proved to be highly successful with the attendees and became the first of a regular monthly series of presentations which subsequently addressed additional separate subject matter on each occasion, researched by us in response to being proposed by the national sales manager.

Basically the tool-kits that we provided led an innovative and highly orchestrated and standardised dialogue between the sales person and their target prospect. The initial focus was on determining which service or product might be appropriate. Next, based on which product or service was identified, the mini expert system generated a series of questions which enabled target customer responses to be entered into a spreadsheet. This input was then acted upon using a range of formulae which led into the preparation of a base Total Cost of Ownership (TCO) / Cost Benefit Analysis summary in line with parameters enabling a range of 'what-if' scenarios so that the results could be 'tweaked' and the potential 'value' subsequently presented to the prospect customer.

This technique enabled both the sales person and the target to work together – in a highly professional way - but most importantly to now illustrate and concentrate attention on potential 'value' as opposed to price.

The key turning point came after an initial two months when the sales manager told me that based on our input more of his sales staff turned up at those monthly meetings that we addressed than ever before for his own internal sales meetings! The sales people felt more effective, confident and professional. In fact they were. They could now effectively differentiate their sales approach and technique against their competition.

QED!

Without going into further detail, we began to receive a range of invitations to propose for new business including an initial multi-million dollar supply chain rationalisation project which our bid was eventually awarded against our own major competitor and the client's incumbent supplier!

In my fishing parlance there is value in considering how at relatively low cost you can win new business by using a sprat to catch a mackerel!!

Another moral of the story: Never lose sight of the implications and potential of isolating and demonstrating 'value'.

# Getting to 'Yes' – Overcoming Objections to the Sale

There are any number of techniques and approaches to help win a sale but one of the simplest that I have come across, particularly if the customer or prospect is proving to be difficult to pin down towards what might be termed the 'end game', is as follows.

As long as you know the real needs of the client and you are sure that:

> (i) you have a solution that represents a good fit; and

> (ii) you can establish both the solution Value Proposition and your unique USP; and

> (iii) you are actually dealing with the key decision-maker.

get to a point where you are confident that the client really understands what you are offering. Then ask for the business. At this point if the client seems to be unsure or uncertain, or appears to be backing off; ask the question – 'what are your major concerns and objections to proceeding with my proposed solution'?

Get the client to actually establish each concern – making a note of each and try to understand what priority each concern has in the client's mind. Get the client talking, under no circumstances interrupt the client. When you are certain that all objections have been spelled out and you understand the priorities, ask the following key question – 'if I can adequately address each of your concerns / objections, do we then have the basis for the deal?'

The logical and in fact psychological client response to your question is more than likely - 'yes'. Now you have the basis of re-establishing your proposition highlighting how each objection / concern is fully addressed and associates such with unique value. Quietly lead the customer through this process. Simple but very effective.

# The Customer Agrees the Sale – Say Nothing

I learned this little sales technique some years ago when working with one of the world's great enterprises. It's extremely simple but quite regularly amazingly effective, in fact essential.

You have worked hard at securing a business sale and now you are in the prospect's office having summarised your value proposition and you hope that the prospect is ready to agree the deal (which you hopefully have painstakingly gone through to satisfy every last detail) – or better still, is ready to sign the contract. You then state – 'so we now have a deal?'

Say nothing more. Keep absolutely silent. Wait until the prospect says 'yes'. Then shake hands. Then, say nothing. Keep absolutely silent and let the prospect speak first. (Should the prospect still indicate some reluctance, stating some objections, proceed as in the previous chapter to isolate the objections).

In the majority of times human nature will drive the prospect's behaviour in terms of making a statement justifying their decision to proceed. Only after the prospect has spoken and confirmed a 'yes' can you respond with a remark such as – 'thank you for putting your confidence and trust in my proposition and in me'. Or something of a similar sentiment.

Now you can be assured the deal will in all likelihood go through.

There is a lot of psychology involved here. If you should speak first after shaking hands it is highly likely that if there is any feeling of concern on the part of the prospect it will be raised then. Any number of questions are likely which could jeopardise the deal irrespective of the fact that a handshake has taken place. Try it, it works and can save a lot of disappointment and loss of time.

Once again - Simple but highly effective.

## Squash, Bowling & Customer Relationships

If you consider the basis of an initial business relationship it is more than likely that it involves only one or at best a small few personnel from each side. Certainly this is a dangerous place to be if the business is essentially only involving one individual from each side. Consider the impact of a resignation or a falling out!

I have always tried to ensure that after an initial sale is signed and you are now in a supplier / customer relationship, I build a significantly wider set of contacts and inter-relationships.

If the nature of your business allows, a very simple way to do this is to use social activities. For example, you might have a group of squash players in your business, so invite the customer to field a team and organise a squash evening at the local courts. You make all the arrangements and put on a supper and drinks at the conclusion of the games. Suddenly you have commenced to widen your sphere of influence (certainly you have extended some points of contact) across the customer and have created a significant level of new relationships – between your personnel and the customer's. Using this approach also enables you to further promote a sense of teamwork within your own organisation as well as the creation of significantly more 'bonding' with the customer.

The range of opportunities to apply this to is very wide – bowling, soccer, five-a-side, basketball, netball, karaoke, etc, etc.

Now that introductions have been made it becomes very easy (and in fact a natural consequence) to get dialogue going across a wider range of contact points across both organisations. From time to time this is also going to identify new opportunities.

It is important that you create a 'relationship map' so that you can see at a glance who in your organisation has the capability of contact with members of the customer's personnel. Also very important that when contacts are made they are subject to oversight so that the overall relationship is properly managed.

The approach also allows you to create a very simple means of further contacting the customer – thanking them for participating, 'hope you enjoyed it and – oh by the way perhaps we can schedule to get together to discuss that other piece of work that you mentioned'. This type of interaction gets around all the normal issues of having to make a sales 'cold call'. Most importantly it also serves to begin to differentiate you from the competition!

Also by extending the 'points of relationship' between you and the customer in this way, you start build a more rigorous model which can play directly into a TAS Relationship Map.

# Brand & Branding

Firstly, some key elements that need to be engrained within your strategic thinking.

Branding is the art of building and constantly reinforcing market perception – and then living up to that perception – in perpetuity.

Branding is both the exercise which provides the 'umbrella' and the environment for:

(i) an internal organisation-wide focus for all events and activities – in fact everything that the organisation 'breathes' and

(ii) (ii) every interaction with every part of the target market(s) and segment(s) that the organisation needs to and wishes to influence.

Branding is impacted by the perception generated at <u>every</u> touchpoint influenced directly by the style and culture of your organisation, your people (and everyone associated with you – that includes distributors, partners, franchise holders etc.). It overlays, permeates, implements, reinforces and endorses perception.

Brand will be a significant driver of superior business performance. Specifically, it contributes to overall shareholder value.

The creation of brand value can truly be measured. Thus, if it can be measured – it can be managed. If it can be measured then its value will become a significant element in the valuation of your entire enterprise. Of key consequence if you are merging, acquiring or selling your business or looking to raise funding – particularly within a share issue.

Brand delivers much more than a product or an image – it drives the entire customer experience. And when the experience is the 'brand', brand management underpins the entire organization. By virtue of this, your enterprise must engage in a fully committed to and coordinated approach. The approach must align operations, functions, processes and procedures to create the culture required to sustain brand 'promise'.

Just by way of a simple example – National Geographic is recognised internationally as media of quality. They began and continued with the provision of market information contained in a simple yellow bordered rectangle. Even to this day, if we see that yellow rectangle we immediately recognise both – National Geographic and have an anticipation of quality.

Virgin is another good example. My view is that they encapsulate what I would call 'radical innovation'. As an aside, I once sat next to a Virgin executive on a long-haul flight. We discussed that given the power of their brand they could migrate business into virtually any arena. Tongue in cheek I suggested that based on their brand value they should definitely get into Media. I suggested that their provision of a global news feed which would contain solely positive news would go down extremely well and be fully differentiated. My thought was that a title of 'Virgin on the Ridiculous' might attract a bit of attention!

Returning properly to the subject, branding is the product of a multiplicity of events, issues, activities and achievements. It does not happen overnight but rather is a cumulative process, and once the required brand / image is obtained[9] – must be continuously reinforced.

In many respects the nature of brand / image is not only the product of orchestrated activity but becomes dependent on the very culture of the organisation itself – and vice versa. In fact – a virtuous circle.

Some focus areas for consideration:

- How the launch of new products or services can capitalize on existing brand and thus positively differentiate themselves from the outset;

---

[9] This requires very accurate assessment and is referenced further in Voice of the Customer – VOC.

- The need to utilize brand to dispel any customer doubts as a potential barrier to uptake;
- The need to continuously exceed market needs for information;
- The imperative to optimize brand to consistently create a highly favourable 'value proposition' in the minds of existing and new customers;
- The need to always fully ensure internal staff, external resellers and distributors comprehensively 'live the brand'.

Brand strategy should never lose sight of two key tenets:

I. The need for focus on 'what matters to the customer';
II. and ultimately, that you – your organization and your people – are the brand.

Brand constitutes your 'promise' to customers upon which they can always rely on to guide their choices.

Branding should never be confused with Marketing, or in fact Advertising. These elements are the mechanics by which we convey particular messages, or perceptions, to target audience(s) / market(s) / segment(s). For example if your target segment is Active Youth / Lifestyle, then 'Cool & Exciting' might be the message or needed perception. Professional / Business Corporate segments might emphasise Quality, Excellence or Solution Oriented.

Marketing and Advertising must be very carefully considered - so that every piece of output which 'touches' the targeted market or segment carries the appropriate reinforcement of segment brand as illustrated above and in addition applies the overall experiential perception of – Value.

In summary, branding is totally comprehensive in respect to its demands across the entire organisation so that a branding campaign and its associated organization-wide permeating processes must be literally 'owned', as well as really understood, led and managed.

Experience confirms that a branding plan is necessary to enable a full understanding – by everyone, of the variety and potential extent of activities that need to be scheduled, owned and managed; and to set expectations and enable measurement of progress and performance.

Here is a sample checklist of activities or focus areas that can be used homogenously and in an integrated way to create and continuously reinforce your brand 'message':

- Advertising
- Advertorial
- Awards & Prizes
- Big Events
- Blogs
- Breakfast Sessions
- Briefing Sessions
- Booths at Conferences & Exhibitions
- Merchandise
- Newsletters & Briefing Notes / White Papers
- Editorial
- 'How To' Guides
- Introductions / Prefaces to, or reference in Business Books
- Involvement in Hosting National / International Events / Conferences
- Issues Papers & Thought Leadership Pieces
- Letters to the Editor
- Market Research Reports
- Media Kits
- Media Round-tables and Lunches
- New Product / Services Launches
- Newsletters
- Podcasts
- Scholarships / Bursaries
- Schools Essay Competitions & Awards

- Special Interest Group (SIG) Formation
- Sponsorships
- Standards Publications
- Statistics & Trend Reports
- Success Stories & Case Studies
- Trade Statistics Compilation
- TV and radio appearances
- Year Books & Annual Reports
- Etc; etc.

How much are you going to put into your selection of branding activities and focus areas?

# Voice of the Customer – VoC

The term 'Voice of the Customer' links to much of the material already addressed in previous chapters. Simply put, it describes techniques and methodology to establish exactly what your customers think of, and might be saying about, your business and its products and services. This enables you to address both specific customer and generalised customer base views to enhance customer retention and associated customer lifetime value - as well as providing analysis of the need for mitigation activities where dissatisfaction exists.

Most importantly it can drive the necessary customer-centric culture across your entire organisation. Follow the link below to get an initial and useful overview, not only of methodology but also of a couple of interesting case studies.[10]

As previously addressed, you can't manage what you can't measure, thus ensuring that you have an accurate and realistic understanding of your customers perception of your interactions with them is vital.

Accessing and assessing customer feedback on a 'how are we doing' or 'how can we improve meeting your needs and expectations' basis is something which essentially should be highly focussed as well as being both dynamic and continuous - as opposed to running a once a year or generic customer questionnaire.

It seems that many organisations who have introduced an online 'chat' facility seem to regard that this type of customer interaction (emulating voice contact) as bringing them closer to the customer – but as we have all experienced, an almost instantaneous link to lists of online FAQs doesn't do much for enhancing the relationship – rather it further emphasises their approach to reducing their own costs! The approach also appears to be part of a wider strategy of attempting to identify

[10] https://www.qualtrics.com/uk/experience-management/customer/voice-of-customer/?rid=ip&prevsite=en&newsite=uk&geo=FR&geomatch=uk

where there might be opportunity for upselling or cross-selling promotion of other products or services (both their own and their associates!) — in its own right not such a bad idea but certainly not focused on enshrining their absolute focus on 'loving <u>you</u> the customer to death'!

# Customer Relationships - Why Fly-fishing Can Be So Important?

There's a difference between fly-fishing and other forms of fishing. It seems that generally the uninitiated perceive fly-fishing as more of an arcane art. Actually it is! I've found quite regularly that if I'm in discussion with a customer or potential customer and I mention that I am a fanatic for fly-fishing, from time to time the response is – 'I would very much like to learn that'.

This then allows me to say that I would consider it a great pleasure to act as a teacher and guide. And there you are - you suddenly have the beginning of a relationship that basically has nothing to do with business but will potentially cement a long-term connection with that person throughout your business association.

Another aspect of fly-fishing is the stress-relief and relaxation component. If you are running a business there is a real need to take time for yourself to relax and unwind and to give yourself the opportunity to think lots of things over – without interruption. There is nothing quite like being part of nature, by a river, stream or lake and hunting the elusive trout (or salmon). In fact a good number of species in both salt and fresh water are very attracted to the fly! I highly recommend it for enabling a positive and productive decision-making process. It's good for the mind but it's also good for the soul! Sometimes you even get a meal out of it!

However, it doesn't have to be fly-fishing, in fact it can be any topic or pastime which can engender a one on one interaction with the customer.

# Competition

## Aligning With Strategic Giants

A lot of my early business experience was involved with software development, developing applications for specific vertical industry users. As a small business the costs of initial development were already highly significant in terms of personnel and equipment costs as well as normal overhead. If contracted to develop a solution directly for one client then of course specific costs could be recovered or defrayed, but if attempting to design a generic solution that could be marketed to a wide market, then overall costs were much more and a wide range of other factors were brought into the equation.

The underlying issue to consider was one of scale and how to create it. Not only to enable addressing the widest possible market but to do so in reducing or negating the impact of competition.

In order to mitigate the issue, I found that the most appropriate approach was to interest vendors of the equipment types that the solution would run on, getting them to assess the market potential for the sale of their equipment which would be hosting the application that we would develop; i.e. enabling for them the opportunity to sell a complete combined hardware / software solution. This also enhances the vendors' overall value propositions.

In this way we arranged that the equipment vendor companies would make available development equipment to us on a gratis or loan basis. Additionally, they would assume the sales / marketing role, freeing us of that. In certain cases we could negotiate commissions for each sale of their equipment as well as receiving the licensing costs of our software.

As the equipment companies were huge, multi-national organisations, our positioning, aligning with them, provided a scale and competitive profile that was not possible with us working in isolation. And of course, it also gave us access to a range of capabilities that we could not possibly emulate in our own right, as well as the potential for additional revenue.

The subject matter doesn't have to be software, any product or service that in combination with a large vendor enhances both organisations' positions.

There is scope to assess a wide variety of synergy-linked relationships irrespective of the industry or market you are in.

Certainly worth thinking about.

# A Way to Neutralise the Competition

When you are in the early stages of running your business a key issue, in fact regularly a problem, is your lack of scale. This is particularly important with regard to your ability to compete against large and entrenched opposition. In fact in most cases, any competition.

The previous chapter proposes a particular strategy of aligning with synergy-linked large organisation partners.

Another simple way that I have developed to overcome the negative impact of competition is to firstly segment your targeted market(s) by competitor. (It should actually be already evident and refined within your Strategic and Business planning).

If you identify competitors of the same size and capability as yourself, analyse which might be susceptible to an approach in terms of extending an opportunity to work together. You would be surprised that not only does this sometimes produce a very 'two plus two equals a number greater than four' situation but can also lead ultimately to conventional mergers and acquisitions.

Where competitors are significantly larger or in fact smaller than yourself, analyse their positioning relative to their potential fit with yourself and also in fact, their positioning against <u>their</u> own larger competitors. Attempt to identify where your capabilities might enhance their sales success and approach them with your element(s) that might further differentiate their efforts.

Once again you might be surprised at the positive response and potential outcome of doing such based on the potential opportunity coming to them as it is from left field.

If the idea is adopted and you go ahead, both sides benefit.

If the idea is rejected, at worst you might establish a few more insights into their organisation. Either way, you benefit.

# Recipes for Project Success

# The Customer is Always Right??? Oh Really!! Then Why Do So Many Procurement Projects Fail?

This is a really fascinating subject, particularly in respect to IT projects (although in reality it is just as prevalent in other types of project) on which volumes have been written. Interestingly enough the volume of text addressing the subject has yet to reduce the number of disasters and their concomitant wastes of time, resources and money.

I describe the situation in terms of analysing what can regularly occur within IT procurement, an area in which I have had a lot of involvement. However, a lot of the learning is equally applicable to a wide range of other product or service procurement projects.

In my experience the root causes of project failure can be summarised under the following headings – each obviously necessitating a very strong mitigation strategy; certainly these are not exclusive or exhaustive:

- Lack of customer senior management buy-in / senior management sponsorship;
- Inexperienced customer management;
- Users of new systems who do not really know what they want;
- Internal politics and the existence of entrenched and conflicting positions;
- Poorly stated solution specifications / requirements;
- Poor project management;
- Project solutions selected on price and not on total cost of ownership (TCO) or value.

This list is not in priority sequence. In most cases a combination of root causes exists. Taking each heading in turn:

**Lack of customer senior management buy-in / senior management sponsorship:** In just about every project there is a need for various parts of the business to combine their resources and certainly pull together within an agreed plan. The various parts of the business generally represent differing silos of personality, culture, vested interest and competence. Invariably there is friction, even turf wars. This situation must be mitigated and the only way to achieve that is for over-arching senior management to buy-in to the project and be prepared to step in at any juncture to secure and ensure accord. In this sense ensuring that every project has the appropriately senior 'sponsor' is vital. That comprises one half of the need, the other half is the very real requirement for accurate and objective project management of progress being reported (particularly to the project sponsor) in a previously agreed format and to an agreed timetable. Over and above scheduled reporting, additionally the link between project manager and project sponsor must be totally dynamic enabling immediate communication of any concerns as well as the intervention of the sponsor if and as required.

**Inexperienced customer management:** It fascinates me how, in so many cases, new management hires are brought in to critical and senior management positions and projects when they really have no right to be there. CVs can be made to look the bees' knees and embellished with glowing references from a past employer. Generally the hirer never stops to think that maybe the glowing reference was created in order to be rid of that person! If you are engaged as a consultant or as an advisor to a project where it becomes obvious that specific decision-making and management capability are sub-optimal, it is essential that this is communicated to the project sponsor and appropriate recommendations for mitigation are provided. Notwithstanding the above, there are numerous examples of where existing customer management personnel really don't have the appropriate experience and are completely out of their depth but obviously very loathe to admit such. From experience as a consultant and advisor to a range of procurement projects I have learnt to take steps to quickly and discretely establish the capabilities of the management involved in the project oversight as well as the management and users directly involved in specifying, implementing and using the sought-after solution. A way of approaching this also accommodates the following heading.

**Users of new systems who do not really know what they want:** This is very common. It becomes critical when the solution user specifications and parameters are provided to vendors within an RFI / RFP situation. At the very least this issue provides for potential sub-optimal cost benefit / value over time as well as potential lack of fit to a greater or lesser degree. Generally, cross-sections of users might establish basic needs and requirements but have little or no understanding of how a solution (particularly a tech-based solution) can provide and enable a wide and diverse range of additional features and benefits elements that they are not aware of or have not considered.

A very simple but effective approach that I have found works well is described in the next chapter – Optimising RFI & RFP Procedures.

**Internal politics and the existence of entrenched and conflicting positions:** It would be a rare occurrence to find an organisation in which friction does not exist between business units or departments. Such can be based on personalities, perceived position in the pecking order or attitudes that consider certain business activities more important than others. If this scenario is encountered it is essential that the project sponsor is informed and acts to introduce a teaming environment as soon as possible. In certain conditions there can be scope to bring the key management and users together for facilitated team building activities either on or off site. In either case it is always appropriate to have the project sponsor address the group at various stages to ensure that everyone is 'singing from the same hymn sheet'.

**Poorly stated solution specifications / requirements:** This heading is common enough, created through various conditions from lack of knowledge through to lack of interest or lack of experience / ability or a combination of all. The worst example I have ever come across was a half-page used by a senior manager project initiator to describe the needs and outcomes of a multi-million dollar global solution – worse still, written by the one senior line manager with no input involvement at all with the managers of the other business units affected. All this in a multi-billion dollar organisation! The best way to address such a situation is described in the following chapter. As an objective advisor I recommend an approach to subliminally (without users losing face) enable the building of knowledge and understanding of both current and future potential solutions through a series of no-obligation vendor presentations. Once these vendor presentations are delivered, both management and users can then re-visit and re-confirm their stated needs based on their increased awareness of what the market has to offer.

**Poor project management**: In the same way that you would not wish to go to sea in a boat for a journey captained by someone with very limited experience, getting the right level of competence to manage and steer a procurement project is vital. This is not really the time to attempt to learn by experience! Sometimes (in fact more often than not) this calls for bringing in someone from outside the organisation, specifically with significant and relevant experience, along with testimonials from previously successful assignments. There are many project management methodologies but the key over-riding elements from experience are that the project manager selected must have empathy with the range of personnel involved in the project and must be capable of developing confidence as well as the ability to relate effectively with the senior project sponsor.

**Project solutions selected on price and not on total cost of ownership (TCO), true cost-benefit or value**. There is a lot of difference between a perceived initial price tag and the overall true Total Cost of Ownership (TCO). In order to establish true cost, and thus the overall cost benefit, it is essential to be able to identify and then quantify the wide range of associated costs over the proposed economic lifetime of the solution. Notwithstanding financial accounting measures, particularly depreciation, you should consider most of the following, and in certain business areas, additional elements relative to the nature of the business. Consider the following over the agreed complete economic lifetime of the solution / asset:

- Departure from incumbent solution vendor(s) costs
- Licensing costs
- Contractual rise and fall costs (CPI)
- Potential legal costs
- Staff Training
- Potential changes to staff costs (i.e. hiring new skills)
- Implementation costs
- Maintenance costs
- Support and Service Level Agreement (SLA) costs
- Eventual replacement or upgrade costs
- Environmental issues
- Security
- Backup
- Downtime insurance

Only when you have ascertained the combined financial impact and inter-relationships of the above, will you be able to establish the true benefit / value of the investment.

# Optimising Request for Information (RFI) & Request for Proposal (RFP) Procedures

Most regularly, users don't really know what will constitute the most appropriate / ideal solution. User needs across the organisation will be subject to a range of priorities and specific wish-lists.

Where an organisation-wide solution is being considered – for example a replacement or new customer service or contact centre solution – there is a strong likelihood that very few, if any, users will be aware of what new or latest technology solutions exist. An excellent approach to address this is to firstly obtain a broad list of needs from users and then prior to publishing an RFI, arrange a series of no-obligation presentations from appropriate vendors (five or six market leaders generally suffice). You will find that vendors will likely jump at the opportunity to present.

The brief given to the vendor presenters is to establish what solutions they currently have available and what is in development in the near-term and thus to enable users to understand what really is the current 'state of the art'. The presentations should be facilitated and made interactive, allowing all the users and management involved to contemplate how particular solutions could really further enhance their future business as they currently contemplate it, as well as meeting their considered existing and currently stated future needs.

This process expands both management and users' understanding of what is available and builds a valuable knowledge base. In many ways this additionally starts to build a 'future proofing' element for the solution. Most importantly it enables building a much wider set of the attributes (specifications / requirements) that a new solution might address and include. Apart from the commitment of time, the approach enables the organisation to build knowledge and understanding without cost. The knowledge building cost essentially being absorbed by the potential vendors. The approach moreover enables a significant but subliminal competence building and non-threatening education of users.

Once all vendor presentations have been completed, re-visit the users and now get them to establish a renewed set of specifications. Have them list these in an xl spreadsheet column with each allocated a priority in an associated column. The priority can be established as a colour code – green for 'must have'; orange for 'would be nice'. Note here that various users (business units) across the organisation will have differing priorities for various solution features, so each user or business user type must be segmented and allocated their own distinct columns.

Publish an initial Request for Information (RFI) to the market including the annotated xl as above. Ensure that the document is in accordance with internal legal procurement guidelines. Within the RFI, ask responding vendors, in addition to summarising their approach as text in their proposals, to annotate in a distinct column within the provided xl spreadsheet their solution fit against each user requirement, once again using a colour coding: green for 'fully meets requirement'; orange for 'partially meets requirement'; and red for 'does not meet or address requirement'.

Once the RFI responses are received, the colour coding provides an initial 'at a glance' level of fit. Both the user and vendor colour codes can now be represented / substituted by numeric values and in this way an initial table of comparative fit against requirements can be established as well as a table of comparative rankings regarding the viability of each vendor. It also serves to identify numeric scores against each user's / stakeholder's / business unit's prioritised needs. (Remembering of course that various users will have different requirements and priorities). Vendors can now be invited to run a presentation of their formal RFI response which allows users to establish an even stronger understanding of fit and potentially a re-marking of vendor responses.

At the culmination of all vendor presentations a finalised table of comparative rankings regarding the viability of each vendor can be prepared upon which a shortlist of two or three can be invited to respond to a full Request for Proposal (RFP).

The subsequent RFP process can then be entered into using exactly the same methodology and format as applied within the RFI to enable an understanding of the most appropriate level of fit across all users. However, the RFP considerations must also include provision of all the necessary timeline and financial parameters to enable the creation of true total cost of ownership (TCO) and the associated cost benefit analysis (CBA).

In proceeding as above, as previously mentioned, don't lose sight of the fact that various stakeholders will have different sets of requirements. Don't simply add all the rankings to establish potentially the 'best' vendor. There could well be a case that particular stakeholder needs are not adequately met whilst others are and this really must be reconciled before any award can be made.

# People, Performance, Recognition & Reward

## Invest & Reinvest in People – Permanent Staff

The majority of businesses will require you to build up a staff of varying capabilities and competencies. In my own experience a significant part of my workforce were technical types; programmers, analysts, project managers, consultants and the like apart from support and administrative staff. Add to this the need for sales and marketing staff, personnel / HR capabilities, secretarial, legal, line management, etc, etc.

Having invested both time and money in attempting to attract the very best and brightest, it is both necessary and logical that you want to retain their services for as long as possible – not only to get a return on your investment but to consolidate around a stable team. In my case I required both permanent staff and a contract labour force and I was particularly concerned to avoid the latter workforce adopting a mercenary attitude towards the company. In essence I treated my permanent staff and contractors (addressed separately later) in a similar way.

Firstly, I obtained market surveys which outlined the salary and wage rates (overall remuneration) in my market. I always made a point to pay in the upper quartile.

For permanent staff I researched what other benefits were contained within an overall 'package'. I made a point to ensure that the combination of elements within the overall 'package' could be readily identified as being consolidated in the upper quartile. Conventional elements included:

- Paid holiday leave
- Paid sick leave
- Maternity / Paternity leave
- Special / Compassionate Leave
- Staff Events / Social Club
- Car / Travel Allowances

- Annual training / skills development
- Personal development training
- Health insurance

Additionally, I looked at involvement in a staff pension fund (discussed later in a separate chapter) and a bonus system. I also developed what I termed 'Wizard of the Week Awards' – an approach to incentivise and reward work 'above and beyond' expectations, which I also discuss in a separate chapter.

I wanted all my permanent staff to be assured that there was a future for them in the business and certainly inviting them to participate in the company pension scheme after a qualifying period (six months) tended to differentiate my company from many of my competitors.

A key ingredient in approaching remuneration as above was to provide regular six-monthly reviews against a set of mutually agreed key performance indicators (KPIs). Also discussed separately later.

I wanted my people to really understand that we were hiring for the long term and that not only were remuneration issues a key concern but also staff and personal development. In the latter case at review time, a key component was a mutual assessment of what further education and training was necessary in terms of both the current role undertaken and future aspirations but also skills development requested by the staff member per se.

I always liked to establish the value / cost of education / training / staff development as a percentage of the overall package and ten percent as a minimum seemed to work well. This subject was always a key element of every staff review.

# Invest & Reinvest in People – Contract & Freelance Staff

In respect to my contractors, I developed several considered 'left field' approaches.

I prided myself on attracting the best and brightest contractors. Not only individuals who were highly capable but individuals who could and would act as 'flag-bearers' for the company.

Once allocated to a customer project I would make arrangements to visit them on the customer sites as often as possible. They could provide a mine of information regarding the state of the customer: outstanding problems, staff issues, project progress and very importantly, opportunities for our company to identify and fill further client needs. Of course the other aspect of visiting them on site would allow me to consistently reaffirm their importance to the company and reassure them of my genuine interest in keeping them 'in the fold'. Another element of these site visits would open up opportunities to meet with the customer manager involved and discuss issues and possibly new opportunities.

When new opportunities surfaced via the contractor, I would always organise a bonus in their next pay cheque as recognition.

Another aspect of my relationship with contractors was to invite them, and also pay them the time, to attend our regular monthly staff meetings. The meetings were timed to last an hour at the end of the day followed by drinks and some socialising. I wanted to make my contractors feel very much part of the business. In fact all my contractors were always invited to our staff social events and customer events.

Perhaps the most radical element of my contractors' relationship was to provide a measure of continuity. Continuity of revenue being the major concern for any freelancer / contractor.

Because the business was developing software on a range of computers in-house, I had the capability, if the contractor's skillset matched the in-house requirement, to offer contractors an opportunity to join in-house project teams once their external contract had completed if there was no immediate new contract available to start. The rate of pay would not be the contractor's conventional remuneration but a payment relative to the project they would be working on and the team in which they would be working.

This approach very much mitigated against creating a mercenary attitude on the part of the contractors – i.e. always searching out work from the highest bidder in a competitive market. It brought them closer into the company culture and in fact over time, quite a number of contractors asked to join the permanent staff. We gladly took them on.

The approach also worked in reverse from time to time so that full-time staff could leave the payroll and join the ranks of the contractors.

# Nest-egging Pension Fund Contributions

I have always been in favour of creating compensation packages which both reward people for and encourage their longer term commitment. A key element within remuneration has been the availability of a staff pension plan, made available after an initial period of six months from date of hire.

I have also been in favour of working directors joining the scheme and making monthly contributions.

The structure of the pension arrangements I favoured established a facility for each staff member to opt in or otherwise. If opting in, a percentage of an individual's salary would be deducted at source monthly to be paid into the fund which would be administered by a reputable specialist organisation, usually an insurance company. The business would initially match the individual's contribution. Over time the company, at its option, could contribute further percentages. In certain environments there are tax benefits to the overall arrangement.

The rules that we would establish regarding pay-out entitlement were centred on providing a sliding scale of percentages of the company's contributions in addition to the individual's contributions in accordance with the number of years the staff member served the business. The sliding scale of employer contributions paid acted directly as an incentive for personnel to stay for longer periods of time.

Obviously if a staff member left the business prior to reaching the 100 percent attainment of employer contributions, the residual amount of employer contributions remained in the fund, earning interest thus enhancing the overall value of the 'pot'. The entire fund value also earned interest. The rules established quantified what if any amounts of interest on employee contributions would be paid out if the individual left the scheme.

Thus over a period of time the fund becomes an excellent savings account.

On closing the pension scheme, say in the case of selling the business, the entirety of the fund after distribution of staff entitlements is available to the participating directors who have been set up as 'owners' of the scheme. In certain jurisdictions this can be a favourable tax exempt windfall.

In summary the use of a pension fund does serve the interests of both employer and employee alike.

# 'Wizards of the Week' Awards

Everyone needs to understand their worth. When in business and employing people the worst thing you can do is take their contributions for granted or appear or be interpreted as to be doing that! The outcome spawns dissatisfaction and essentially creates a mercenary workforce. My approach to recognising effort (notwithstanding establishment and monitoring of staff Key Performance Indicators (KPIs), regular six-month staff reviews and the use of an 'always open door' policy) has delivered excellent esprit de corps and increased commitment over a long period of time. I eventually termed it the 'Teamwork Principle'.

The way I have approached the issue is quite simple. I would hold and chair a regular monthly meeting to which all staff and contractors would be invited. (In fact contractors would be paid at their hourly rate to attend). We would hold the meeting on the last Friday of each month unless there was a holiday in which case we would use the next available Friday.

The monthly meeting was a means to provide everyone with an update of our progress during the past month – new business won, office / admin details and updates on a range of staff / contractor and social issues including introductions to new hires. The session would never last more than hour before drinks were served and an atmosphere created for everyone to socialise in a relaxed environment.

However, prior to concluding the session there would always be what I termed the 'Wizard of the Week' awards. A misnomer really as the awards were monthly but 'WOTW' rolls off the tongue much easier! There would generally be one such award, sometimes several based on what 'over and above' work effort had been noticed and appreciated during the month. We would also encourage all our people to nominate candidates for the award(s).

The awards would be both quantified and personalised according to the extent of the effort and also the particular needs of the individual. Thus, a staff member about to be married might receive cash towards a honeymoon, someone moving house might have their removal expenses paid. One time our CTO had put his back out and so we bought him a special ergonomic-designed armchair. We always tried to customise the awards which I believe indicated that (a) we really noticed and appreciated the efforts and (b) personalised the award to indicate the fact that we were truly a caring employer – not only for the individual concerned but also importantly for their 'other half'.

We had an extremely good reaction from all our people. It did provide a special differentiation to the approaches taken by other firms and I believe contributed a great deal towards the loyalty of our people and the very minimal staff turnover we experienced. This was particularly noticeable within the ranks of our contractors. They stuck with us like glue!

Another issue was the fact that we encouraged nominations for awardees from their peers as well as their management which is a key factor I believe, in the creation and maintenance of a strong 'teamwork' ethos and culture.

An appropriate quote:

*"Treat your men as you would your own beloved sons. And they will follow you into the deepest valley." Sun Tzu, The Art of War.*

## Staff Reviews

I don't believe that there is just one perfect way in which to review a staff member – basically it should be determined within the overall culture of the organisation.

In a 'teamwork' oriented environment there is plenty of scope to interact with staff dynamically and to identify any specific issues that need to be addressed sooner rather than later. Nevertheless, a structured review approach is necessary to enable the linkage between progress, performance, recognition and reward (remuneration).

The basis of Staff Reviews should, in my opinion, consider five specific elements:

   I.   Regularity
   II.  Two-way street
   III. Follow-up
   IV.  Key Performance Indicators (KPIs)
   V.   Peer Assessment

Most importantly the reviews should be scheduled to specific dates and adherence to those dates is essential.

However, remember that there is huge benefit in not only reviewing the performance of the staff member but obtaining feedback as well. Turn the formal review into a two-way street and obtain insights that might otherwise be lost. In this respect I have found that a review has always worked best for me if I deliberately make it conversational as opposed to 'confrontational'!

In addition to addressing expectations of performance, there is great benefit in establishing an employee's aspirations of career development and the staff review is an ideal opportunity to isolate what training / education might be scheduled for the individual over the upcoming year

– not only from the company's point of view but also from that of the staff member – in terms of <u>personal</u> development.

Once the review has been completed ensure that full follow-up of all the issues agreed to during the review takes place.

In respect to Key Performance Indicators and the introduction of Peer Assessment are concerned, the following two chapters address each in turn.

## Key Performance Indicators – KPIs

In several sections of this book reference is made to KPIs, initially when building your Strategic and Business Plans and subsequently when managing day to day business – however they are particularly important in respect to managing your people.

It is a basic right of a staff member to fully understand what exactly is expected of them. In fact I consider the application of KPIs when it comes to staff performance as vital for both the company and the staff.

The establishment of metrics is essential if you are going to be able to measure progress and performance. You can't manage what you can't measure.

I have always believed that on initial hiring and with regularity thereafter, an employee should be given an appreciation of what the company requires and expects and that the process of discussing KPIs should be a two-way / mutual exercise. It being vitally important that the individual talks through, understands and feels comfortable to commit to the agreed metrics - which should always be written up - with a copy provided to each party.

If the staff review cycle is six months then the KPIs should be measurable over and at the culmination of that period of time and the staff review should establish a discussion on how those KPIs have been met or otherwise. Meeting the expectations of the KPIs can then be the basis of delivering on a range of promises that might impact role, remuneration etc. Conversely lack of achievement can be discussed and hopefully measures put in place to bring the performance up.

One international organisation that I worked with for a period of time would set KPIs and then review six monthly on the basis of:

- Far exceeds expectations
- Sometimes exceeds expectations

- Meets expectations
- Sometimes fails to meet expectations
- Fails to meet expectations.

Comparison against these criteria would establish next-step career development for the individual concerned. Two consecutive reviews at the 'Far Exceeds' level would generate wide interest in the individual across the organisation. Two consecutive reviews at the Fails to Meet level would invariably lead to advice to seek alternative employment.

When it comes to Sales personnel it is often seen that the term KPIs is replaced by the term 'Sales Target' or 'Quota'.

Obviously, it is imperative that both the company and the Sales staffer mutually agree on what sales revenues can and will be brought in but I believe that it is just as important to consider, and where feasible, establish other measurable criteria for example:

- New Customer Creation
- Existing Customer Retention
- Existing Customer Growth
- Favourable Customer Survey Inputs
- Team Involvement
- Mentoring and Teamwork Capability
- Progress through the development of the TAS 1-20

All of the above are very capable of being converted into both revenue creation and cost reduction numeric values.

In summary, KPIs enable the monitoring and measurement of progress across a wide and diverse range of activities across the business over an agreed timescale.

## Using Peer Review Groups

When in the early stages of the business development I always tried to conduct the initial staff reviews myself. These would be very much two-way sessions and the key foundation was the mutually agreed prior set of Key Performance Indicators (KPIs).

Eventually the business would grow so that the number of staff reviews I could be involved with reduced significantly and those that were undertaken were with the higher echelon of my senior management, overall reliance on the conducting of reviews instead placed on line management.

However, in any event I selected particular staff to form what I termed a 'Peer Review Group' and as a small team, they would conduct a performance review of related staff members in addition to my own involvement or that of line management.

I would also use this approach when interviewing for hiring new staff.

The Peer Review Group would bring significant understanding of the day to day capabilities and performance requirements of the individual, not just in terms of work output but also involvement within the overall team, degree of comfort with the culture, need for further training etc.

The selection of the Peer Review Group would not be based on title or seniority, it could include a variety of positions including even new recruits and trainees.

I would expect to sight a summary report from the Peer Review Group which would be added to the personnel file of the staff member appraised and if required I could thus identify and act on any issue that had been raised as a concern or also intervene, notify or be involved, in the event that promotions and other considerations be followed through with.

I found that the approach generated a very interesting and positive 'sense of ownership' not only with the reviewee but also the reviewers.

Another positive element of the approach was the extent of objectivity injected into staff appraisals. The approach obviated any personal issues.

There should be recognition that the approach does create an additional burden on staff and impacts in a minor way on their total of productive hours to a degree. However overall, I found it well worth the effort.

# Teamwork

## The Power of Teamwork

From the very beginning of my involvement in creating my own businesses I have had an intuitive feel that 'Teamwork' should be the foundation for the business per se and the philosophy of all those people involved in the business. I also wanted my customers to evidence that we wanted to work <u>with</u> them as opposed to just <u>for</u> them.

Teamwork culture generates a need to be open with everyone involved in the business, whether this drives the approach to customer interactions, to regular staff meetings, the layout of the office environment (which I insist on being completely open plan) or the informal adaption and adoption of project and development methodologies such as Agile[11] – discussed further shortly but footnoted below for further reference, which I encourage you to follow up.

I have always created what I term as an 'Open Door Policy', which I encourage my line management to also adopt. Essentially physically keeping close proximity to staff within the open office environment and being available for discussion on any subject dynamically during the day. If I need quiet time or have a need for a meeting and not be disturbed then I would use a room set aside for that purpose. Otherwise I would always be available for interaction.

Obviously, I would set aside a Boardroom for specific closed meetings and also reserved for customer presentations.

I would extend the 'teamwork philosophy' to address the style of approach we would adopt in the development of a product or in fact the running of a project.

This approach in product development would see the creation of small teams constructing identified small elements or components in what has widely been addressed subsequently in formal methodologies such as

---

[11] https://www.atlassian.com/agile

Agile or Lean. Essentially breaking down a complex end-product development into 'bite-sized' incremental tasks and proceeding with further development only once the incremental component end-product is obtained. This also enables a consistent feedback cycle to customers and once again supports the 'teamwork' culture. Additionally, it can allow the development of elements in parallel across separate teams and obviously enables a more manageable early warning situation rather than encountering an impasse across an entire complex solution only when completed, if the solution then ultimately fails.

Another approach adopted within the development of projects was to encourage and engage an openness within the ranks of team members to speak up at any time that they identified a better way of approaching things, or could see improvement or cost reduction opportunities. This approach also led into the recognition and reward environment created and as discussed earlier in terms of 'Wizard of the Week Awards'.

In this regard I was interested to study the Japanese approach to what is termed 'Kaizen'[12] and saw how it had been (and still is) adopted in a diverse range of companies to both promote 'teamwork' and pride of ownership as well as enabling enhanced productivity and the identification of efficiencies.

In the naming of various businesses I have generally incorporated the word 'teamwork' because I want to emphasise with customers and potential customers that I want to work with them. That in combination with their people and capabilities we can produce a highly valuable outcome that fits with their philosophy and culture. I believe that the psychological impact of this approach resulted in the winning of many projects on a differentiated basis against my competition.

---

12

https://www.investopedia.com/terms/k/kaizen.asp#:~:text=Alex%20Dos%20Diaz-,What%20Is%20Kaizen%3F,a%20gradual%20and%20methodical%20process.

In the thirty and more years since I first incorporated 'teamwork' in my approach to business I have seen the term used almost universally. It seems that it does have universal appeal – and more importantly can generate some spectacularly successful results.

# Negotiations

# The Power of Honesty and Openness in Negotiations

Imagine - you might be on holiday in a backstreet market somewhere in the third world and discussing the purchase of a souvenir of some sort. The shop-keeper you are negotiating with has never seen you before and the likelihood is that he will never see you again.

It is possible that the shop-keeper might be the most honest person you have ever come across but that is not highly probable! (No disrespect to back-street market traders!) He knows that you are a tourist and will likely never see you again. There is nothing to lose in 'negotiating' with you and anything might be said to conclude the sale. Mindful of this you part with your money, trusting that you are not being too badly overcharged and hope that your purchase will continue to perform as expected but if not, you are not going to be too upset. However, if the worse does happen you might laugh it off (depending of course on how much you were charged) but for sure you will never likely do business with that person again. More than likely you will relay your experience on to a number of people and certainly you will remember the experience for a very long time! Exactly the same goes for any business deal that you are involved in – wherever in the world or whatever the circumstances.

In business your focus and responsibility is on winning the confidence of your prospective customer and thus winning the sale – but then, <u>retaining that customer for as long as possible</u>. In that respect, unlike our friend above, you have everything to lose. If that prospect or customer thinks (rightly or wrongly) for a moment that you are not being totally honest or open, or even gilding the lily or exaggerating – both during the negotiation or subsequent to the sale – you will lose that business and the customer for ever. As previously referred to, a lost customer who departs with a negative view is highly likely to influence a number of other prospective customers' purchase decisions adversely.

There is no substitute for complete honesty and openness when in discussion with your customers or prospects. Regardless of how anxious you are to conclude the sale. Always deflect 'difficult' questions for which you don't know the answers with a standard response – 'good question, I'm not sure of the answer but I'll find out and come back to you as soon as possible'.

In the above context we are focusing on negotiations in a customer setting but the same goes for any dealing within business and particularly when in discussions and negotiations with funders, business associates and especially your staff!

# Approaches to Negotiation

Before we get going on this topic, be aware that there are numerous courses and tutorials on the subject and I would encourage you to 'google' the subject and see in depth what is available.

For our purposes I would like to introduce you to what I believe are the 'watchwords' to consider when faced with your own involvement with negotiation.

**Human Chemistry Relationship**: It is very important that there is empathy between you and the party with whom you are negotiating. If you believe that the right level of relationship doesn't exist, then select another of your team with whom the other party can feel comfortable.

**Honesty and Trust:** As important as relationship, there must be a very strong element and understanding of openness, honesty and trust. Without that, each proposition you put forward will be regarded with suspicion.

**Value Proposition**: The party with whom you are negotiating must always have identified the value in the deal you are proposing. If not you are wasting everyone's time.

**Objectivity / Put Yourself in Their Shoes:** Make every effort to understand where the other party is coming from. What are their needs of the proposal you have put forward and what are their needs of what they would consider a successful outcome of the negotiation? If you can get to a point where you know exactly what they would declare as a successful outcome, then you just have to work towards that goal if it complies with your needs of the deal. On that basis you are no longer negotiating or to the prospect customer it may appear so!!

**Win / Win**: In any negotiation there are only three outcomes. One party wins at the other party's expense (win / lose); both parties come away with nothing or have conceded too much (lose / lose); or the goal that you should be striving for – an understanding for each party that they have each gained something (win / win). Sometimes declaring this approach up front can steer the negotiations towards a successful outcome. It is likely that if the above headings have been complied with and you have analysed what concessions you could make – or can alternatively demonstrate and convince the other party that you are making concessions – the negotiation will be successful.

**Emotions**: One of the worst things that can happen in a negotiation is where personalities take over, tempers rise and the atmosphere for negotiation becomes toxic. Adopting a style of approach considering the above headings, you can see that your most appropriate approach tends towards being professionally dispassionate. Should the other party introduce a negative environment, act immediately to suggest a time-out so that both parties can consider their next steps.

**Silence Is Golden**: Whenever you sense that the negotiation is becoming bogged down or tense as a result of the other party's reluctance to accept or consider a condition, create space in the discussion by becoming silent, letting the other party speak first. Alternatively suggest a time-out. Quite regularly a concession can be made at this point to move the negotiation forward. Better if the other party makes the concession!

There are volumes of material available on the 'art' of negotiating. I strongly advise that you put time and energy into research and hope that by introducing the topic now it can become the catalyst for your further skills development.

## Negotiating – Black Hats & White Hats

Sometimes it seems as though the negotiation is going nowhere. It could be specific sticking points in the deal or possibly the personality of the people involved.

Here is a technique that I have used quite successfully to make progress to secure the deal. It necessitates that prior to the actual negotiation you have established a strategy based not only on what concessions might be made but on bringing in an 'alternative' negotiator who you have declared to the other party at the outset is on your negotiating 'team'.

It could be that you are sticking to what you have put forward as non-negotiable elements of the deal. The other party is steadfast in not accepting such and is becoming exasperated with your positioning. At this point you vacate the discussion and in fact the room and your 'alternative' takes over. He or she immediately apologises for the stance that you have been taking and suggests that he / she will see what can be done and perhaps get a position to move forward if some sort of concession can be identified. He / she then works carefully forward to identify, obtain or put forward a required concession using a personality that is in direct contrast with the stance that you have been taking.

It's basic psychology that the other party will sense an environment in which they suddenly feel more comfortable / that they have achieved a 'win' and the emotions and personality issues that have previously held up the deal become that much easier to overcome!

# The Power of 'Open Book'

This insight was developed and applied when asked to assist a facilities management company in their bid to retain their largest and most valuable client. As in many cases, an existing long-term relationship with automatic contract renewals had made my client the service provider a little lazy and their customer felt that they were not receiving the appropriate level of attention and value from the contract. Based on this my client's customer went out to the wider market and requested my client - the incumbent service provider - to bid anew on a fully competitive basis!

The service contract had run for many years based on price with annual provision for price increases subject to changes (usually rises) in the Consumer Price Index (CPI).

In order to now differentiate my client's competitive bid (and win back the heart and mind of their customer) I suggested that we proceed as follows:

Firstly, we created a template in which every product or service provided was broken down into all of its constituent elements. For each element we established the associated actual cost of provision including a percentage of the service provider's overhead costs (licences, computer costs, rent, payroll, etc). In essence a descriptive activity based costing (ABC) model. Where savings were identified against the existing services provided or where alternative ways of working could be applied, these were documented also.

We then researched the global market in terms of identifying and corroborating the extent of margin that was being applied in the facilities management market. Gartner Group assisted in this activity. This percentage was then added to the base cost of provision of each of the services requested.

The third element was to create an initial set of Service Level Agreements (SLAs) in which particulars were stated for what levels of service and performance were going to be provided and the associated financial considerations and procedures warranted in the event that such were not attained.

The combination of these elements were clearly stated in the re-bid and for the very first time provided a real understanding of the true costs and inherent value – not only for the customer but also for my facilities manager client!!

Additionally, information was provided in an attempt to detail the additional potential costs (logistics, legal etc,) should the customer decide to migrate away from my client's service provision.

The provision of this level of information was a real eye-opener for my client's customer and in fact enabled them to provide updates to their RFI / RFP documentation sent to vendors to now enable a like for like comparison should they so decide. Interestingly enough, an opportunity on which they declined to act!

The result of the re-bid was a direct win for my client. Not only this but the introduction of a much improved management insight (for both my client and their customer) into the costs and profitability of their service provision. In parallel, a highly professional portrayal of the provision of services on which their customer could clearly see and understand the value of the contract.

Most importantly it introduced an entirely new basis of relationship between my client and their customer – a relationship that truly exemplified both professionalism and trust.

The bottom line – everyone was a winner!

# Miscellaneous Tips & Tricks

## Optimising Your Commute

For many years I lived an hours drive (on a good day) away from my office. I never felt that this was a burden or a waste of precious time. Certainly the commute enabled me to enjoy some quiet personal time and also to think through issues that needed attention. In the evenings, the drive allowed me to unwind so that I was ready to be a relaxed (and hopefully energised) family man on my return home. As it happened my journey took me past some beautiful ocean scenery and I could pull up for a short time and take in the view!

Anyway, the message that I would like to impart in this chapter is a very simple approach to using commute time productively. I kept a small tape recorder in the car and as and when I had a constructive thought about the business I would record a memo to myself to follow through later. I would also record memos to my secretary and to team members via my secretary. On arrival at the office, I would pass the mini cassette tape to my secretary, she would give me the tape from the previous day and so the cycle would continue.

Using this approach, I could optimise my time. It ran in parallel to making and receiving telephone calls. It also allowed optimising my secretary's time. All up a very simple productivity booster.

Obviously an alternative approach is to use digital means but often times not that practical or safe when driving a car!

# Nervous about Public Speaking? – Then Try This

Quite by accident I finally, after many years, came across the means to quell my nervousness when having to do public speaking, provide an important business presentation or give any address to a large gathering e.g. at a conference – particularly the latter.

The first pre-requisite is to prepare your presentation and to become absolutely confident that it addresses the subject matter and that you can deliver it without hesitation. Be confident that the presentation is appropriate and well researched. Try it out on a colleague, friend or family member.

Nervousness regarding your delivery usually starts the day before your presentation and builds up to a crescendo late in the evening, worsening through the night and into the early hours. By the time you are due to take the podium and deliver your presentation, your worst fears have eventuated.

The way to combat this is to deliberately <u>not</u> try to go to sleep the night before but instead go to bed with a really good book, something of the un-put-downable type. Keep reading until you cannot keep your eyes open. If you do end up fast asleep and then wake up again in the early hours, don't re-visit your presentation but instead go back to your book and keep reading for as long as possible before having to get ready to leave for the presentation venue.

At the venue ensure that your presentation materials are all in order and delivered and aspects such as projection are checked out. If there is a foreign audience, check that your presentation is with the simultaneous translators. Remember that your delivery should be a bit slower than normal if it needs translation. Use larger than usual font size and double spacing. Stick <u>exactly</u> to the script given to the translators. This is essential! Any deviation will cause chaos for them. I'll give you a humorous example of that later.

Now you have done everything that is required. The fact that you have had less sleep than is normally required will have little or no impact. You will have short-circuited the progressive build-up of stress and anxiety and your delivery will be an enjoyable activity.

Try it and see.

Of course there is always the old favourite. I can't remember who dreamed this one up but basically the idea is to imagine that your entire audience is naked. Sort of puts any potential embarrassment or nervousness on them, not you!

# The Art of War – Messages For Business

The Art of War is widely regarded as the essential analysis of successful military activity, written by Sun Tzu reputedly in the fifth century BC! It is acclaimed for its insights into tactics and strategy and in this regard has often been regarded as a basis for decision-making processes that are equally as appropriate in business.

Some quotes:

*In the midst of chaos, there is always opportunity.* Highly relevant in the global COVID pandemic situation. Recently published were the financial results of one of the larger vaccine producers – 36 billion annual profits!

*To know your enemy you must become your enemy.* This can be interpreted in terms of really understanding your customer or target client as with the application of a Targeted Account Selling TAS 1-20 profiling – discussed in an earlier chapter.

*He will win whose army is animated by the same spirit throughout all its ranks.* An insight into the needs of a business requiring to be united in terms of strategy, tactics and teamwork; i.e. a business whose personnel are 'all singing from the same hymn-sheet', united by a common culture and mission.

*Treat your men as you would your own beloved sons. And they will follow you into the deepest valley.* Being totally responsible for your people. Ensuring that your people are consistently rewarded fairly for their effort as well as additional recognition and reward for over-achievement and working above and beyond expectations. I related my own approach to this in a previous chapter.

*Ponder and deliberate before you make a move.* A serious recognition of the essential need to plan and align your business approach as realised within the techniques and methodologies of Strategic and Business Planning, addressed earlier.

***Success in warfare is gained by carefully accommodating ourselves to the enemy's purpose.*** Further recognition of the need to truly understand the nature of the customer or targeted client's business objectives and particularly being able to address their burning or hot issues.

***Strategy without tactics is the slowest route to victory. Tactics without strategy is noise before defeat.*** The consideration that for all of the planning that might be undertaken the real key is establishing how your strategy will be put in place and what are the metrics and key performance indicators that you create to continually assess exactly how you are pursuing your objectives. Remember, you can't manage what you can't measure.

***Hence in the wise leader's plans, considerations of advantage and of disadvantage will be blended together.*** This relates particularly importantly with regard to the SWOT or Strengths, Weaknesses, Opportunities and Threats elements of your Strategic Planning. Not only from an initial or once annually revision but in a regular and dynamic analysis of your business environment and your positioning and capabilities.

There are many other very salient and sometimes obvious connections between military tactics and the business of running a business. Research Sun Tzu and discover more for yourself. In any respect it is an interesting diversion[13]!

---

13

https://www.goodreads.com/author/quotes/1771.Sun_Tzu#:~:text=%E2%80%9CAppear%20weak%20when%20you%20are,strong%20when%20you%20are%20weak.%E2%80%9D&text=%E2%80%9CThe%20supreme%20art%20of%20war,subdue%20the%20enemy%20without%20fighting.%E2%80%9D&text=%E2%80%9CIf%20you%20know%20the%20enemy,will%20also%20suffer%20a%20defeat.

## Making Friends With The Media

One particular activity that I orchestrated on an irregular basis was an invitation to a cross-section of media contacts to come to my boardroom for a few drinks after five.

However never under-estimate the consumption characteristics of the media. Make sure you have enough alcohol on hand so as not to run dry before the event concludes!

The basis of the session would be a short welcome and a distribution of a folder with a few press releases and company / business activity updates. Once some initial alcohol had been consumed it became increasingly simple to steer a conversation around what the business was achieving and in fact generate simple discussions on the state of the industry, the market etc; as well as general chit chat, including asking the media what were their views on a range of issues.

The most important element was that, although irregular, I would put on drinks for the media on several occasions throughout the year. They had an expectation of the session and looked forward to it.

It also helped to further differentiate me from the competition.

It encouraged a more personal and friendly relationship which then engendered calls from various media looking to me for a quote or an opinion. In this way as a small company we created a disproportionate amount of media coverage which built a significantly wider perception of our presence in the market for both our existing and potentially new customers.

Using the technique proved much more successful than attempting to interest the media just by sending them press releases and hoping for the best.

In essence we became a logical and easy 'go to' source for inputs on a wide variety of industry matters. For their part the media achieved marketing results for us dis-proportionately higher than the cost of the alcohol they consumed!

Keep it in mind, I highly recommend it.

# Never Get Lost in Translation

There are three basic elements to consider when discussing translation:

- Language,
- Culture and
- Phonetics.

I have travelled extensively internationally on business and have been involved in numerous business discussions where there was a reliance on the use of third party provided simultaneous translation. Additionally, I have had many business meetings where I had to rely on the English language skills of the people I was meeting.

Unfortunately, apart from my mother tongue of English, my language skills are poor to the extent of being dangerous!!

I remember once being at an international conference on the subject of international joint ventures. An Australian industry speaker took the podium and commenced with an ad lib as follows (try if you will to set the beautiful tonality of the Ozzie accent in your mind): 'Well, g'day, international joint ventures are very much loike love and marriage. First you have the initial meeting and courtship. Then you have the engagement and finally the marriage. But just as in love and marriage you have to understand that sooner or later someone is going to get screwed'!

A golden classic in my view. However, the very large Japanese contingent hadn't got a clue and were totally reliant on the skills of their simultaneous translator, who had no prior warning of the ad lib and for reasons best known to her either declined to translate the profanity or could not and so she simply said 'all Japanese should laugh now'. There was a spontaneous and hearty uproar that lasted for a full minute. Even funnier than the original statement!

I was once speaking at a conference in South Korea to a huge audience in a massive hall. As I settled myself at the podium I ad-libbed the fact that I was from New Zealand, a country of three million people and fifty million sheep. You can imagine my surprise (read shock and bewilderment) when the entire audience burst into raucous laughter. Unfortunately the pre-printed text of my speech as given to the simultaneous translator did not contain the opening ad lib. She thought that I had said something humorous, didn't quite catch the meaning and so directed the audience to do the polite thing – and laugh! Just revisiting the moment fills me with dread!

Apart from language, there is another critical component to understand – that of culture. In the Western world if we hear the word 'yes', we assume that the outcome is positive – 'yes, the deal will go through'. However, in many countries, particularly in Asia (China, is a very good case in point), there is a strong emphasis on not offending and thus it can be quite common to hear the word 'yes' even accompanied by a handshake when the real situation is 'no'!

It's simple – there is a huge reluctance to disappoint and to avoid you losing face. Likewise it could well be that you are making an arrangement with the CEO but in actuality it could well be the family grandmother or matriarch who has the final say!

And on the cultural issue, just imagine how many differences there are from country to country: we wave goodbye, in India they wave hello. In countries such as France and Italy they embrace and kiss on both cheeks. Try doing that in North Korea!

Moral of the story – always check out nationality, social mores and business etiquette.

And, as a postscript, let's consider the phonetics and accent elements of language. A friend is of a non-English persuasion, conversant in several languages but with a nearly but not-quite-complete English vocabulary. From time to time I am amazed with some terrific interpretations, each of which could be feasible technically but have totally different meaning in actuality.

Two of my favourites:

(i) An interpretation of the theme music from the movie Ghostbusters. Hearing the music as played on the radio and singing the chorus not as 'who you gonna call – Ghostbusters' but *'who you gonna call – those bastards'!!* And,

(ii) Kenny Rogers song 'You Picked a Fine Time to Leave me Lucille' – not 'four hungry children and a crop in the field' but *'four hundred children and a crop in the field'*.

Priceless!

## Political Risk

As mentioned in the Preface, I have been involved over many years in a range of international development projects. One of the most interesting aspects – and certainly involving the most significant personal time, energy and money - was developing a high-tech based retail and wholesale hypermarket project requiring massive investment and being sponsored by the nation's vice-President!

The basis of the project was to build new tech-oriented retail and wholesale market infrastructure and to commence a highly developed technology-enabled supply chain based initially on the delivery of New Zealand agricultural products. A major upskilling element ran in parallel, designed to run in conjunction with the State University school of business.

However, it all came to nothing when initially the country's President and Vice President fell out and our project, our hard work, innovation and enthusiasm (and particularly our sponsorship, investment and support structure) disintegrated into nothing. In parallel to the internal political side of things, we were seriously let down by the international Development bankers who had agreed at the outset that they would fund the entire project once initial milestones had been met! Should definitely have got that in writing!

Collectively the entire episode is certainly worthy of a book or two in its own right and maybe one day it might happen! Who knows, the opportunity for the project might re-surface one day! But it goes to show how much fate, destiny and timing can all impact what business you are in.

Never forget that. Also keep in mind how sensible it can be to buy political risk insurance!

## Academia – Your Development Partner

From time to time I was presented with a need to resource specialist skills quickly or for a specific project. Sometimes the very nature of the skillsets required made the identification of suitable people quite difficult in the open market.

What I did discover though was the availability of considerable depth of capability within the academic and research institute environment. In fact I eventually developed a strategic approach to build contacts with a number of universities as an adjunct and an extension of my own R&D facilities.

I found that there was a very strong willingness in academia to make skills available at very realistic and cost-effective pricing. In fact in a particular circumstance I was subsidised by Government to explore the creation of R&D contracts with universities and research groups.

Not only was I able to access the appropriate level of skills required but I also had the additional opportunity to identify possible and eventual new hires into my organisation without personnel or head-hunter agency costs!

As a number of projects that I became involved in required the creation of consortia (typically within the EU), relationships with particular universities and research institutes became additionally valuable.

I would suggest that it is an area well worth while considering.

## Academia – Your Talent Hatchery

Here's an insight regarding education and the availability of personnel from personal experience.

Over a number of years in one of my early businesses I hired a good many new recruits. Typically, in those early days, I would base my hiring decisions mainly on intuitive feel but I would also look closely at academic achievements but initially focus on university graduate hires. However, I found that new graduates entering my workforce seemed to have a disproportionately high opinion of themselves and didn't integrate well with my growing band of street-wise, eccentric geniuses. (This is a personal view not a generalisation!).

I opted to experiment by initially hiring a couple of polytechnic students for their holidays. I was very surprised at their extremely high levels of commitment to learn, to follow instructions and the dedication that they demonstrated. We enjoyed this phenomenon for their six to eight week vacations which essentially served as a rapid assimilation internships or micro-apprenticeships. Come their graduation, we offered full-time employment. It was one of the smartest things we did. These guys worked well over and above requirements and consistently far exceeded expectations. They became long-term members of the team, loyal and a credit to the company.

Could have been good luck, but food for thought nevertheless!

## Knotty Problems

From time to time you need to become totally focussed on how to unravel a particularly nasty problem. A knotty problem. Sometimes even called 'a can of worms'!

Well, this is where fishing experience really comes into play. Not so much the 'worms' part but certainly the 'knotty' part.

Occasionally when fishing, the line over-runs and leaves the spool too quickly or is snagged on a tree or caught around a submerged root, or who knows, even a very large fish which breaks your line just at the wrong moment. When you pull at the line with all your might you suddenly are confronted with a 'bird's nest' – a real mess.

Basically, good fishermen (fisher persons just doesn't sound right and fisherwomen sounds downright rude!) are patient souls. They have to be to stand in freezing cold water for hours on end or braving the elements waiting for 'the moment'.

The trick to sorting out a huge knot of fishing line is four-fold:

- get comfortable (you could be doing this for a while!);
- work slowly;
- tease out the tight mess into as large an area as is possible – make the line as loose as possible;
- consider calling in some help – you know, just like your mother or grandmother used to get someone to position their arms just so she could create loops of her knitting wool.

After a while the puzzle becomes more obvious and you can decide whether or not ('knot' - pardon the pun) you will proceed further or abandon the effort.

In business this can illustrate a point. If you are confronted with a real knotty problem get into a quiet space in which you can consider all the issues.

    i.    Don't allow external pressures to impact the way in which you will consider the issues;

    ii.    Stay cool, calm and collected;

    iii.    Be patient!

    iv.    Try and remove all or any time pressures;

    v.    Start writing down as many of the elements of the problem as you can possibly think of. Consider the various issues and their relationships to each other independently;

    vi.    Don't make the mistake of trying to tough out the problem alone – think about bringing in some other objective and constructive points of view and assistance but only once you have fully considered point (v) and can clearly illustrate the issues.

You will be surprised that what at the outset appears to be a huge problem without a solution can regularly turn into something quite different. Very often a negative situation can have a very positive outcome.

I find that this approach also assists in clearly defining when an issue should be abandoned or identifying what I would call 'the do nothing' option.

Of course, the more time you spend fishing the more patient you will become. Which is a real bonus in any event!

## Why Are Some Senior Recruits So Useless But Have Incredible References?

Have you been in a hiring situation where a new senior hire steps into your environment and immediately starts to make you wonder what the hell they are talking about. This is generally in parallel with demonstrating an attitude that is nothing short of overbearing within a nasty air of feigned superiority. Alternatively you may be working on a client project and come across the same type of individual.

Well, it happens but why and how?

Simple. There are any number of individuals who have a greater sense of their own importance than is deserved or exists in reality. Over a period of time these types of people really start to generate a self-assured self-belief and start looking for rapid career growth. Generally their current employers have had quite enough of them and counsel them to the effect that they may be better off within a new company with better advancement prospects – ('we would love to keep you but we don't think that we can provide the opportunities that you deserve to advance your career') and on that basis are prepared to provide the most glowing testimonial as to their capabilities to get rid of them.

As part of a new job interview / new hire assessment with such an applicant, (in fact with any applicant), the tendency is to look at the letterhead and signature of the applicant's testimonial and possibly hire on that recommendation or certainly give it some weight in the overall decision process.

My advice. Stop. If something looks too good to be true – it generally is! Firstly find ways if you can to contact other personnel in the applicant's organisation and solicit their views on the applicant to establish the reality around the type of person you think you might like to hire.

It's amazing the lengths organisations will go to, to get rid of personnel that they just can't tolerate any more! Providing an amazing testimonial / reference is the simplest and most cunning approach available.

Beware the new senior hire (preferably still an applicant), so self-assured and clueless with a gold-plated testimonial.

# Sandwich Bar Economics

Going back a number of years, a friend of mine – an accountant by original profession (and in fact one of the very few passionate accountants I have known!) – decided that he and his wife would depart the glamour of a corporate office and open a sandwich bar for breakfasts and lunches in a well-placed site in a business district.

It was around the time when people started thinking about eating good organic food.

The site chosen was ideal, in the middle of several multi-storey office buildings with a very high catchment of well-heeled and hungry potential customers.

In next to no time the sandwich bar generated a very good reputation for wholesome, tasty food and the ambience of the sandwich bar and the very pleasant interaction with whom became very regular customers continued to grow the business.

It was on one day that my friend had a marketing brainwave to encourage new business and possibly even enhance the profitability of the business.

He decided to push the message that indeed, there was such a thing as the possibility of a 'free lunch'!

With so many regular customers on first name and friendly terms and the new marketing concept of an opportunity for a free lunch, he started to offer a new and radical option on the purchase price of lunch or breakfast.

He would ask customers if they would like to flip a coin for the price of their order. Heads they would get a free order, tails they would pay double.

Well, the customers considered that the law of averages would actually mean that in the long term they would at worst break even. So, a majority went for the option.

The cost of making a sandwich would be say one dollar. The retail price of the sandwich would be four dollars. If my friend lost the toss of the coin, his loss would be one dollar. If he won the toss he would get eight dollars. If he lost ten times, his real loss would only be ten dollars. He would only have to win twice to cover his costs and still make a profit. Interpreting and representing any potential revenue shortfall as a marketing expense and considering the value of the sales gimmick attracting new customers – he couldn't lose!

It takes a while for the penny to drop!

The customer, working on the law of averages, could lose five times out of ten and pay forty dollars. In winning five times the customer pays nothing. Overall the customer breaks even.

In parallel my friend working on the law of averages and winning five times on ten flicks of the coin, will generate forty dollars – the same revenue on selling ten sandwiches at their regular price of four dollars!

Thus if the law of averages enables him to win even less than half the time, the cost of this sales gimmick in attracting new customers to my accountant friend is extremely affordable – everyone wins!

The 'campaign' generated interesting additional customer rapport, it enhanced customer retention and even achieved the goal of attracting new customers.

Applying your own innovative version of 'sandwich bar economics' in a sales campaign can make sense. It could be the basis for a campaign of your own!

It also proves how occasionally some accountants can be quite inventive buggers! Worth remembering.

# In Conclusion

## Murphy's Law

According to Murphy – if things can go wrong – they will!

It's a fact!! There are any number of issues that can silently creep up on you in business that despite your confidence and enthusiasm will conspire to frustrate your optimism!

The trick of course is to minimise or better still negate Murphy by trying to isolate all the possible things that could go wrong.

That will never happen of course and coincidence, good luck and timing will always play a major part in all your dealings. However, do try to consider at least the following – not only in your original Strategic Planning but dynamically as your business proceeds:

**Succession Planning**: Consider the impact of losing key knowledge and skills and develop a fall-back position. Also, consider your own health and abilities! Consider 'Key Man' insurance for yourself and your people.

**Regulatory Changes**: Never be surprised by the changes and chaos that Governments and other authorities can wreak across the business environment. In this respect keep it in mind but basically - just do your best!

**Political Risk**: As detailed previously!! Consider purchasing insurance particularly if conducting business out of your home country.

**Exchange Rate / Currency Fluctuations**: Totally out of your control unless you hedge or purchase forward.

**Climate:** Sounds strange to include but these days is becoming more of an issue - consider the impact of earthquakes and other natural disasters caused by weather.

**Pandemics:** What to say?

# Let's Step Back and Think About Social Media for a Minute

At a loss for something new to read I bought 'Zucked' by Roger McNamee. I recommend it to anyone, both existing social media devotees or those considering. As someone who has spent a lifetime in technology but consistently avoided immersing my entire personal life, contacts and thoughts in social media, I received a frightening endorsement that I had probably done the right thing!

The extent of private and personal information that the current billions of social media devotees are prepared to make available for the gain of completely unknown third parties – that they have probably never, ever considered - is frightening. Likewise, their potential exposure to predatory activity both personal and financial. The fact that money is being made in enabling that is very much a consideration.

The very nature of social media does not guarantee retaining personal confidentiality. The extent to which hackers do harm and will likely continue to do harm by prying into your personal life – is frightening.

On the one hand used in a myriad number of ways, social media is a major means of getting your marketing and brand image messages across. On the other hand a potentially dangerous environment enabling access to nearly everything about you.

Deployer or User. Your call!

## And Finally....

As the great Joe Walsh has enshrined in rock music: "If you act like you know what you're doing, people actually think that you do".

The actor Michael Caine – "I have been both rich and poor. On balance I prefer to be rich!"

Golfer Gary Player's response, when discussing his run of wins on the professional circuit as a result of a reporter mentioning how lucky he had been – "yes, it's amazing, the more practice I put in, the luckier I get!"

Seasick Steve: "I started off with nothing and I've still got most of it left!"

"Know the rules well, so you can break them effectively." Dalai Lama

"Business opportunities are like buses, there's always another one coming" – Richard Branson

"If you really look closely, most overnight successes took a long time" – Steve Jobs

"Technology is cool, but you've got to use it as opposed to letting it use you" - Prince

Me: "Remember …. Careful Where You Place Your Trust and Always Get It In Writing".

# Change, Trust & Timing

There's not really a lot more to say on this. It's a theme that runs right through this book.

Be careful out there!

## Some Additional Thoughts......

We all know what is possible and ordinary. Producing the impossible and the extraordinary is what makes the difference. Remember – *'Impossible is Nothing'!* (Thanks to Adidas).

In order to attain your aspiration towards excellence – become excellently focused!

The journey of a thousand miles begins with a single step!

Things always look better in the morning!

If at first you don't succeed, try, try again!

Time is Money!

Boating is a hole in the Ocean into which you pour money. Similarly some businesses!

Customer Focus: I have really tried to make the contents of this book of real value to you. In an attempt to analyse the balance between 'me' and 'you' I checked the following.......

The personal pronoun 'I' appears 250 times in this book. 'Me' appears 216 times. The word 'You' appears 763 times. Not too bad for a first attempt - but certainly leaving room for improvement!

# Value

**The word 'VALUE' appears 83 times in this book!!!**

# Postscript

Throughout my involvement in business, and in the technology industry in particular, I have had many adventures. I have witnessed at first hand the way that technology develops to permeate our lives. The immersion in the industry that I have experienced has enabled me to develop very strong intuitive feelings in terms of the direction, the application and value of high-tech advancement. And of the unbelievable and widespread mis-management of technology.

It seems that the world has lost or is certainly in the process of losing its way. Instead of the technology being harnessed for good it seems that the value system has been turned around and we can no longer put our faith in what we see and hear anywhere – we are all now susceptible to the internet's social reach.

Software exists that influences both decision-making and perception based on the representation or mis-representation of positive or negative sentiment analysis – which these days cannot be given credibility due to the massive and growing volume of 'fake news' – thus making the sentiment analysis purposefully and dangerously manipulative! No more old fashioned news that could be trusted but potentially new age propaganda that can be relied upon!

Additionally within industry and business it never ceases to amaze me nowadays how much waste and naivety exists at every level, even within the most sophisticated organisations in terms of their management capability, or lack thereof, to obtain appropriate levels of benefit and value from the application of technology.

For all readers considering the way ahead, stop and think in parallel – how can you access and employ the 'best' technology for best effect alongside how can you achieve your real potential, make a difference and at the same time base your actions on always aspiring to the moral high ground. There is a very strong 'feel good' factor associated with doing just that. However unfortunately it may not always make you money. Your choice.

Technology is neither good nor bad; nor is it neutral. – *Melvin Kranzberg's First Law of Technology*

www.ingramcontent.com/pod-product-compliance
Lightning Source LLC
Chambersburg PA
CBHW071405210526
45465CB00001B/259